THE MINDSHIFT EFFECT

Where Change Management is Redefined
and Leadership is Defined

Copyright © 2024 - Mindy Vail, CCMP, M.Ed.
The MindShift Effect

ISBN: 9798323021543
Published 2024

All rights reserved. No part of this book may be used or reproduced in any manner whatsoever without the express written permission of the publisher, except for the use of brief quotations in a book review.

TABLE OF CONTENTS

INTRODUCTION 9

WHY THE MINDSHIFT EFFECT? 13
MYTHS 14
THE SIGNIFICANCE OF THE MINDSHIFT EFFECT 19

PART 1: UNDERSTANDING CHANGE 21

THE NEUROPSYCHOLOGY OF CHANGE 22
RECOGNIZE YOUR BIASES 28
STRATEGIES FOR EMBRACING & NAVIGATING CHANGE 31
PART 1 REFLECTION 38

PART 2: CULTIVATING A CULTURE OF INNOVATION. 39

DRIVE INNOVATION & EMBRACE CHANGE 40
ENCOURAGE CURIOSITY AND EXPLORATION 43
EMBRACE DIVERSITY AND INCLUSION 47
PROMOTE COLLABORATION AND CROSS-POLLINATION 53
PROVIDE RESOURCES AND SUPPORT 58
BUILD PSYCHOLOGICAL SAFETY 64
PART 2 REFLECTION 69

PART 3: THE ROLE OF LEADERSHIP IN DRIVING INNOVATION AND EMBRACING CHANGE 70

LEAD BY EXAMPLE 71
EMPOWER AND SUPPORT EMPLOYEES 76
REMOVE BARRIERS AND ROADBLOCKS 81
CELEBRATE SUCCESS 86
LEARN FROM FAILURE & REWARD RISK-TAKING 91
PART 3 REFLECTION 96

PART 4: COMMUNICATION MASTERY 97

BE TRANSPARENT AND AUTHENTIC 98
PRACTICE ACTIVE LISTENING 102
EMBRACE EMPATHY 108
ADAPT YOUR COMMUNICATION STYLE 112

PROVIDE CONSTRUCTIVE FEEDBACK	115
BE CLEAR AND CONCISE	120
PART 4 REFLECTION	125

PART 5: UNLOCKING POTENTIAL ... 126

UNLOCK POTENTIAL	127
EMBRACE A GROWTH MINDSET	130
SET GOALS	134
ENCOURAGE REFLECTION AND FEEDBACK	141
INVEST IN PERSONAL DEVELOPMENT	147
INVEST IN LEADERSHIP DEVELOPMENT	150
PART 5 REFLECTION	154

PART 6: STRATEGIC PLANNING ... 155

STRATEGIC FRAMEWORK	156
VISION	160
MISSION	163
VALUES	166
STRATEGY	170
PRACTICAL FRAMEWORKS AND TOOLS	171
PART 6 REFLECTION	175

PART 7: LEADING CHANGE ... 176

LEADING CHANGE	177
BUILD A COALITION OF CHANGE CHAMPIONS	180
ALIGN CHANGE WITH STRATEGIC OBJECTIVES	185
INVEST IN CHANGE MANAGEMENT CAPABILITIES	187
MANAGE RESISTANCE AND OVERCOME BARRIERS	191
PART 7 REFLECTION	194

PART 8 – YOUR CHEAT SHEET TO CHANGE MODELS, THEORIES, AND APPROACHES ... 195

PROSCI'S MODEL & METHODOLOGY	198
LEWIN'S CHANGE MANAGEMENT MODEL	201
KOTTER'S 8-STEP CHANGE MODEL	203
MCKINSEY 7-S FRAMEWORK	206
AGILE CHANGE MANAGEMENT	208
APPRECIATIVE INQUIRY	211

PART 8 REFLECTION 214

CONCLUSION: EMBRACE THE MINDSHIFT EFFECT 215

FINAL REFLECTION 218

REFERENCES.. *221*

Change management and leadership development represent more than just organizational strategies — they embody a profound shift in mindset and approach.

It's about recognizing that to impact meaningful change in our organizations, we must first look inward, confronting our own limitations, biases, and fears.

By doing the internal work, we become catalysts for transformation, inspiring others through our example and empowering them to reach their full potential.

Introduction

Welcome to The MindShift Effect, a journey into the heart of leadership development and change management. Whether you are just starting out in your career or you are a seasoned executive, my hope is that The MindShift Effect energizes your curiosity and sparks a positive, productive mindset within you.

Chances are your life has been shaped by a tapestry of experiences — victories and setbacks — all contributing to the person you are today. Whether you're just stepping onto the career path, seeking a new passion to fuel your soul, or you are a seasoned executive satisfied with your achievements yet hungry for more, the pursuit of knowledge remains a constant. Perhaps you're simply striving to be a better person, drawing wisdom from the varied journeys of others. Whatever your story, you've arrived here, and I'm thrilled to embark on this journey alongside you. It is my hope that this book will serve to reinforce familiar concepts while also offering new perspectives to enrich your developmental journey.

For me, all of the above factors formed the foundation and inspiration of this book. As I navigated my own career crossroads, I realized that despite possessing a wealth of knowledge in this particular field, there was still much to learn and explore. The process of writing this book became somewhat cathartic for me, as it compelled me to reflect on past experiences — both personally and professionally. These experiences ranged from the beautiful moments that filled me with joy to the not-so-pretty challenges that tested my patience and resilience.

Embedded within this journey is nearly two decades spent teaching in middle and high school classrooms, an experience that provided invaluable lessons. Transitioning into the corporate world from education wasn't a walk in the park either. I stumbled a lot, fell flat on my face from making mistakes that cost us financially and emotionally. There were moments when it would have been easy to throw in the towel and retreat right back to the classroom. However, I refused to let my weaknesses or fears hinder progress. Each setback became a lesson learned, propelling me forward with determination and resilience. Reflecting on that transformation, I find a sense of empowerment in the ability to adapt to an entirely new environment while drawing from my past experiences. While the classroom brought with it incredible rewards, there were also significant challenges, which included the complexities of parents, administration, and students all trying to find their place in this world.

Subsequently, I entered the corporate world, but one that was franchised. Navigating the complexities of a franchise system presented its own unique hurdles which I lived in for almost a decade. In the franchise system, I encountered a myriad of challenges stemming from its structured framework and decentralized operations. Balancing the need for uniformity across locations while accommodating local variations and strong personalities demanded strategic finesse. Moreover, reconciling conflicting priorities among franchisees, corporate directives, and market demands added layers of complexity.

Amidst these challenges, one constant emerged - human behavior. Understanding the motivations behind people's actions, their resistance, defensiveness, or even argumentativeness, became central. This insight helped me navigate challenging personalities and conflicting priorities with empathy and effectiveness.

All of this was the genesis for this book. For years, regardless of where my paycheck came from, I have always been immersed in the dynamic field of leadership and change management. It's what I love, but it became evident to me that while there exists a wealth of literature on leadership development and change management, many change management methods are highly technical and difficult to understand. They employ complex frameworks, terminology, and methodologies that require specialized expertise to navigate effectively. This can potentially create barriers for those unfamiliar with the field. Much of it seemed to reside in the realm of academia or corporate jargon—far removed from the everyday realities of leaders and change agents on the ground.

There seemed to be a gap—a void waiting to be filled by a resource that was not only informative and insightful but also approachable, relatable, and actionable. For this reason, I'm taking a slightly different, more humanistic, bite-sized approach to change management. I prioritize empathy, communication, and collaboration, aiming to understand the emotional and psychological aspects of change for individuals. My focus is to create a supportive environment to facilitate smoother transitions and garner greater buy-in from stakeholders.

It is also perplexing to me that despite change being an inevitable aspect of life and work, navigating it effectively remains one of the greatest challenges and stressors for individuals and organizations alike. While it may seem intuitive that humans should be adept at managing change given its omnipresence, the reality is often quite different. Change disrupts routines, challenges comfort zones, and introduces uncertainty, triggering emotional responses ranging from anxiety to resistance. Moreover, the pace and magnitude of change in today's fast-paced world can be overwhelming, leaving individuals feeling ill-equipped to cope with the constant flux. Thus, despite our innate resilience, the ability to navigate change successfully requires conscious effort, skill development, and ongoing support. Recognizing the complexities and stressors associated with change is the first step towards building the resilience and adaptive capacity needed to thrive amidst uncertainty.

And so, The MindShift Effect was born—a culmination of years of experiences, learning, and cathartic reflection distilled into a comprehensive guide for leaders and change agents alike. In writing this book, my aim is simple: to provide readers like you practical tools, strategies, and insights that empower you to navigate the complexities of change and lead with confidence, clarity, and compassion, while examining your own perceptions, biases, and behaviors.

Why the MindShift Effect?

This book and my work are about more than just strategies and tactics though—it's about fostering a mindset—a shift in perspective that enables leaders to embrace change, inspire others, and unlock their full potential. It's about recognizing that true leadership is not merely a position or a title but a journey—a continuous evolution toward excellence and impact.

As you journey through The MindShift Effect, I invite you to approach it with an open mind and a willingness to challenge conventional wisdom. Let go of preconceived notions and embrace the possibility of transformation. Whether you're a seasoned executive navigating the complexities of a global organizational change or an aspiring leader eager to make your mark on the world, this book offers something for everyone—a roadmap to success, a wellspring of inspiration, and a catalyst for growth. After all, none of us have all the answers and there's always something new out there to learn.

Throughout the pages of this book, you may notice that certain concepts and themes are repeated. This is done intentionally. Repetition is at The MindShift Effect's core - an essential ingredient for embedding new ideas and behaviors. So, as you encounter familiar themes revisited in different contexts, allow yourself to absorb them, recognizing that each repetition brings deeper understanding and integration of the MindShift Effect principles.

With that in mind, you do not need to inhale this book all at once. It's purposely segmented in chunks, so feel free to come and go, savoring each chapter at your own pace. I also challenge you to go old-school and use the space to write down your thoughts and questions. Let your ideas sit and soak and give The MindShift Effect time to work its magic in your life and leadership journey.

Myths

At its essence, The MindShift Effect embodies a departure from traditional thinking and behavior—an embrace of new possibilities free from old constraints. It acknowledges that genuine growth starts with a shift in perspective, unlocking untapped potential and endless opportunities. To evolve our thinking, we must confront our tendency to cling to outdated beliefs and unconscious biases, clearing the path for transformation. Myths surrounding leadership and change often obscure effective leadership's true essence. See if any of these resonate.

Myth: Leaders are born, not made.
While certain innate qualities may predispose individuals to leadership roles, leadership is ultimately a skill that can be developed and honed over time through learning, practice, and experience.

Myth: You need to be outgoing to be a leader.
There's often an assumption that extraversion is also synonymous with leadership, but this isn't always true. While being an introverted leader may pose its own set of challenges, and while certain leadership styles may appear to lean more towards extraversion, effective leadership isn't confined to any single trait or temperament. Introverted leaders often possess strong active listening skills and a reflective nature for example, allowing them to empower others and foster deeper connections within their teams.

Myth: Leaders have all the answers.
Leadership is not about having all the answers; it's about guiding and empowering others to find solutions collaboratively. Effective leadership involves leveraging the strengths and expertise of others, fostering a culture of learning and innovation, and being open to new perspectives and ideas. Leaders who

acknowledge their limitations and rely on collective intelligence can make more informed decisions and drive greater success.

Myth: Leadership is synonymous with authority or a high-ranking title.

True leadership transcends formal positions of power and can manifest at all levels of an organization, regardless of job title. Leadership knows no bounds—it can emerge from anyone, from the ordinary person to the extraordinary. Just like Foo Fighters' Dave Grohl sings, "There goes my hero, he's ordinary," some of the most influential individuals in my life are those who bear little or no title after their name. They simply radiate optimism, fill the room with positive energy, and possess a remarkable ability to unite people.

Myth: Leadership is a solo endeavor.

In truth, successful leaders recognize the importance of collaboration, teamwork, and delegation, leveraging the strengths of others to achieve collective goals. Even though some leaders may appear to stand alone or make decisions independently, the reality is that the best leaders always have a team behind them. While individual leadership qualities like decisiveness and vision are important, successful leaders recognize the value of surrounding themselves with talented individuals who complement their strengths and compensate for their weaknesses. They understand that no one person possesses all the knowledge or skills needed to navigate complex challenges or drive meaningful change.

Myth: Leadership success is measured solely by individual achievements or personal accolades.

When discussing leadership success, it's often linked to money and status. However, my focus diverges from this. Yes, money is nice but authentic leadership is about empowering others, creating positive change, and leaving a lasting impact on individuals, organizations, and communities.

Myth: Change is usually negative and should be avoided.
While change can be uncomfortable and disruptive, it also presents opportunities for growth, innovation, and progress. Mastering change management is crucial in business, but it's no easy feat. Change, though often uncomfortable and disruptive, also brings with it opportunities for growth, innovation, and progress. Embracing this perspective is key to navigating change effectively in any organizational setting.

Myth: Change can be managed solely through top-down directives and control.
While sponsorship should come from the top, successful change initiatives recognize the importance of involving and empowering employees at all levels of the organization, fostering a sense of ownership and commitment to the change process.

Myth: Resistance to change is a sign of negativity or defiance.
In reality, resistance can originate from a multitude of factors. It may arise from fear of the unknown, a lack of understanding about the proposed changes, or past experiences with unsuccessful change efforts. Effective change leaders recognize that resistance is a natural part of the change process and approach it as an opportunity to understand and they seek to understand rather than take it personally.

Myth: Once change is implemented, the work is done.
Change is an ongoing journey that requires continuous evaluation, adaptation, and reinforcement to ensure long-term sustainability and success. And this is where many change initiatives fail. Despite the considerable effort invested in initiating change, the absence of a comprehensive plan to sustain it can lead to its eventual unraveling. Without ongoing support and reinforcement, even the most well-executed changes can falter, highlighting the critical importance of long-term planning and commitment to change management.

Shifting our perspectives about change and leadership will yield several benefits and throughout this book, I will touch on each one of these myths in detail. By recognizing that change offers opportunities for learning, innovation, and improvement, we can approach it with a more positive and open mindset. This shift in perspective also enables us to navigate change more effectively, as we're better equipped to anticipate challenges, adapt to new circumstances, and lead others through transitions with confidence and resilience.

Additionally, challenging these myths fosters a culture of transparency, collaboration, and trust within organizations, as employees feel empowered to voice their concerns, share ideas, and participate actively in the change process. Ultimately, by debunking myths about change and leadership, we create a more agile, adaptable, and forward-thinking environment that is better positioned to thrive in today's rapidly evolving world.

It's about questioning the status quo, challenging assumptions, and embracing a mindset of continuous learning and growth. It's about moving away from the "because this is how we've always done it" or "we tried that once and it didn't work" mentality. The MindShift Effect invites us to break free from the limitations of conventional thinking and explore new possibilities. It's a journey of self-discovery and empowerment—a journey that begins with a single shift in perspective. This is the essence of The MindShift Effect; it is the realization that our thoughts shape our reality—that by changing our mindset, we can change our outcomes. It is about cultivating a mindset of growth, resilience, and possibility—a mindset that empowers us to overcome challenges, seize opportunities, and unleash our full potential.

Reflect on the myths or misconceptions about leadership and change that you may have unknowingly bought into in the past. Consider how these beliefs may have influenced your perceptions, decisions, and actions in various situations.

By examining these implicit assumptions, you can uncover potential blind spots and biases that may have hindered your growth or effectiveness as a leader.

The Significance of The MindShift Effect & How to Embrace it

According to a recent PwC CEO Insights Survey, 80% of senior executives anticipate that effective change leadership will become even more critical in the next five years, surpassing its importance in the past, an affirmation that change management is more than just a trend. This statistic holds profound implications for how we perceive both ourselves and the world around us. It suggests a recognition among senior executives of the increasing pace and complexity of change in today's business landscape. As such, it stresses the importance for organizations and their leaders to adapt swiftly and effectively to change.

In addition, it reflects a broader societal shift towards acknowledging the inevitability of change and the need for proactive, agile leadership to navigate it successfully. In essence, this statistic prompts us to reconsider our approaches to leadership and organizational management, emphasizing the importance of embracing change as a constant and developing the skills necessary to lead through it confidently.

And as you are probably feeling by now, the significance of The MindShift Effect also extends far beyond the realm of our professional lives—it permeates every facet of our lives, from our relationships to our careers, from our health to our happiness. And remember, this work is not a destination but a journey—a continuous process of evolution and growth. As we navigate the twists and turns of this journey together, may you find inspiration, wisdom, and empowerment in the transformative power of The MindShift Effect, and I'll be there with you every step of the way.

Finally, after each chapter take a moment to consider your mindset, your beliefs, and your attitudes. Reflect on your past experiences, both positive and negative, and how they may have shaped your perceptions. Approach the questions with an open mind and a willingness to be honest with yourself. Remember that self-awareness is the first step towards growth, and by understanding where your mindset currently lies, you can better navigate the path towards transformation and development. No one else knows your inner thoughts and struggles, so you may as well be honest with yourself—no one is judging, and you can't improve if you aren't honest about where you stand.

PART 1: UNDERSTANDING CHANGE

The Neuropsychology of Change

Change is a bit like that unexpected plot twist in a novel or movie - sometimes exhilarating, sometimes nerve-wracking, but it always keeps us on our toes. It's like being handed a new puzzle to solve, except there's no picture on the box to guide us. Yet, despite its unpredictability, change remains a fundamental part of the human experience, shaping our lives in ways both big and small.

Change has a way of unsettling even the sturdiest of foundations. It's like pulling the rug out from under us, leaving us scrambling to find our footing. Whether it's a new job, a breakup, or a sudden move, change has a knack for challenging our sense of stability and security. At the heart of our resistance to change lies the fear of the unknown. The unpredictability of the future can be immobilizing, prompting us to grasp onto the safety of what's familiar and comfortable.

Change can be likened to navigating through a dense fog. Just as the fog obscures our surroundings and makes it hard to see where we're going, change can cloud our sense of direction and leave us feeling disoriented. It's a journey where we're uncertain of what lies ahead, and finding our way through requires patience, resilience, and a willingness to adapt to the shifting landscape. While some people handle change better than others, it's still difficult no matter what, emphasizing the common struggle of dealing with uncertainty and disruption.

Understanding the neuroscience of change and fear provides valuable insights into how our brains respond to unfamiliar situations and perceived threats. At the heart of this understanding lies the amygdala, a small, almond-shaped structure deep within the brain's limbic system.

The amygdala serves as the brain's emotional center, playing a pivotal role in processing emotions, particularly those related to fear and threat detection. When we encounter change, our amygdala perceives the unfamiliar as a potential threat to our safety and security. This triggers a cascade of physiological and psychological responses known as the "fight or flight" response. And although the term "fight or flight" is commonly used, modern research has revealed a broader spectrum of responses to fear, including freeze, flop, and fawn, providing a more nuanced understanding of human behavior under stress.

During this response, the amygdala sends signals to other parts of the brain, including the hypothalamus and the brainstem, which activate the body's stress response system. Adrenaline and cortisol flood the bloodstream, preparing the body to either confront the perceived threat or run from it. From an evolutionary perspective, this response served our ancestors well, helping them survive in dangerous and unpredictable environments. However, in today's world, where many of the threats we face are psychological rather than physical, this instinctual response can often be counterproductive.

In the context of organizational change, the amygdala's fear response can manifest as resistance, reluctance, or outright opposition to new initiatives, processes, or structures. Employees may perceive change as a threat to their sense of stability, competence, or identity, triggering fear, anxiety, and defensive reactions. Understanding the neuroscience behind change and fear provides valuable insights into how leaders can better navigate resistance.

Moreover, by engaging the prefrontal cortex—the rational, analytical part of the brain—leaders can help individuals reframe their perception of change from a threat to an opportunity for growth and adaptation. By appealing to logic, reason, and shared values, leaders can mitigate the amygdala's instinctual response and foster a mindset of curiosity, exploration, and resilience. In essence, by understanding and addressing the neuroscience of change and fear, leaders can cultivate a culture that embraces change as a natural and necessary aspect of growth and innovation. By harnessing the power of neuroscience, organizations can transform resistance into resilience, fear into courage, and uncertainty into opportunity. But it starts with you. As I mentioned earlier, this will necessitate introspection on your part. Let's begin by addressing the ways you tend to default when confronted with fear.

Fight: When confronted with change, do you typically respond with a confrontational or assertive approach, actively challenging the situation or those involved?

Flight: Do you tend to avoid or escape from change, seeking to distance yourself from the source of fear or discomfort?

Freeze: Is your instinctive reaction to change to become immobilized or paralyzed, finding it difficult to act or make decisions?

Fawn: Do you often respond to change by seeking to please others or appease the situation, prioritizing harmony and avoiding conflict?

Flop: In the face of change, do you find yourself succumbing to a sense of helplessness or resignation, feeling overwhelmed and unable to cope effectively?

Why does it matter? While we may like to believe that we don't care what others think, the truth is that to some degree, we should care. After all, these are the people we spend our days with, make decisions alongside, and learn from. How we present ourselves matters, and how others perceive us is crucial to our growth and development. Those who claim otherwise may be avoiding the hard work of self-reflection. Finding the balance between living for others and not caring at all is indeed a delicate endeavor.

While it's important to consider the needs and perspectives of those around us, it's equally crucial to maintain authenticity and prioritize our own well-being and values. Striking this balance allows us to contribute meaningfully to others' lives while also honoring our own individuality and needs, especially in times of stress, when others are looking to you for direction. Understanding how others perceive you as a leader can provide a significant advantage in shaping your career trajectory, so here are some perceptions people may have based on reactions to fear:

Fight: Others may perceive a leader who consistently adopts a fighting stance towards change as assertive and proactive, willing to challenge obstacles head-on. However, they may also view this leader as confrontational or resistant to collaboration if their approach is overly aggressive or lacks consideration for others' perspectives.

Flight: Leaders who tend to flee from change might be seen as avoiding responsibility or lacking commitment to addressing challenges within the organization. While some may view this behavior as a sign of adaptability or a desire to maintain stability, others might perceive it as a reluctance to confront difficult issues or a tendency to prioritize personal comfort over organizational progress.

Freeze: When leaders exhibit a freeze response to change, others may interpret their immobilization as indecisiveness or a lack of confidence in their ability to lead effectively during turbulent times. While some may sympathize with the leader's feelings of uncertainty, others might perceive their inaction as a failure to provide direction or guidance when needed most.

Fawn: Leaders who consistently seek to appease others during times of change may be viewed as diplomatic and empathetic, prioritizing relationship-building and harmony within the team. However, this approach may also be seen as avoiding necessary conflicts or failing to assertively address issues that require resolution, potentially undermining the leader's authority or effectiveness in driving change.

Flop: Others may perceive leaders who exhibit a flop reaction to change as overwhelmed or disengaged, lacking the resilience or confidence needed to navigate uncertainty and adversity effectively. While some may sympathize with the leader's struggles, others might interpret their passivity as a sign of weakness or incompetence, eroding trust and confidence in their leadership abilities.

Some, if not all, of these are likely to have struck a chord with you, whether you envisioned yourself or others as examples. It's natural for such reactions to influence perceptions, which in turn shape people's realities. This is influenced by various factors, such as the context of the change, the leader's track record, and the culture of the organization.

Effective leadership during times of change often involves recognizing and managing one's own reactions while also understanding and empathizing with the responses of others. One reaction is not necessarily better or worse than the other, although there may be situations where one is not as effective based on the impact you are trying to achieve, so recognizing how these reactions can impact team dynamics and morale is crucial as you build your own leadership style.

Similarly, consider your team's dynamics. It's tempting to dismiss or feel frustrated by their responses to change, particularly if they differ from your own. Understand that their behaviors stem from unique experiences and genetics, differing from your own. There's no definitive right or wrong approach; rather, it's imperative to navigate working with diverse personalities if you want to be an effective leader.

Picture a time when you faced a major change, whether it was a new job, a relationship shift, or a big move. How did you react and what impact do you think it made on those around you?

Why do you think you respond to change the way you normally do?

Recognize Your Biases

To enhance our self-awareness around our attitudes and reactions to change, we must scrutinize our own biases, both unconscious and confirmation biases. Because these biases are predominately unconscious, it means that we may not even realize we have them or how they're influencing our thoughts and actions, and without introspection, our interactions and leadership may lack full honesty and authenticity.

Unconscious biases are implicit, deeply ingrained attitudes or stereotypes that affect individuals' judgments, perceptions, and behaviors without conscious awareness. These biases are formed through socialization, cultural influences, personal experiences, and exposure to media and can manifest in various forms, such as racial bias, gender bias, age bias, or affinity bias. They can influence decision-making processes, perceptions of others, and behavior in subtle yet profound ways, often leading to unintended discrimination or unfair treatment. Unconscious biases may influence individuals' receptiveness to change by predisposing them to favor certain ideas, initiatives, or individuals over others based on deeply ingrained attitudes or stereotypes. For instance, if a change seems to fit with what we're used to or helps people we see as similar to us, our unconscious biases might make us more likely to accept and support it. But if the change goes against what we're used to or seems to help people we see as different or less liked, our unconscious biases might make us resist or doubt it.

Similarly, confirmation bias can affect how individuals interpret and respond to information related to change. It permeates our everyday lives, shaping perceptions, decisions, and interactions in ways that can reinforce existing beliefs and hinder objective evaluation of information. People will selectively seek out or emphasize information that confirms their preexisting beliefs or preferences, while discounting or downplaying evidence that contradicts their views. This can reinforce existing attitudes or biases and inhibit openness to alternative perspectives or new information that may challenge the status quo. Conversely, recognizing and mitigating confirmation bias promotes critical thinking, open-mindedness, and informed decision-making.

In essence, unconscious biases and confirmation biases can influence how individuals perceive, evaluate, and respond to change, potentially shaping their level of engagement, receptiveness, and willingness to participate in change initiatives. And while some people may want to believe they are free from these biases, this is impossible from a neurological standpoint; everyone possesses unconscious biases. Neurologically, these biases are ingrained in the human brain through various mechanisms like socialization, cultural influences, and personal experiences. These biases serve as mental shortcuts that help individuals process information quickly and make decisions efficiently. As a result, even individuals who consciously strive to be neutral may still exhibit unconscious biases due to the automatic nature of these cognitive processes. Therefore, it is virtually impossible for anyone to be completely free from unconscious biases.

So, the focus isn't on attempting to eliminate them. Instead, it's about acknowledging and confronting them, enabling them to be advantageous rather than adversarial. We can do this through self-reflection and introspection. Taking time to critically examine our thoughts, attitudes, and reactions can reveal underlying biases that may influence our perceptions and behaviors. Seeking feedback from trusted friends, colleagues, or mentors can provide valuable insights into blind spots or biases that we may not be aware of. There are also bias assessments and structured exercises designed to uncover implicit biases that can help us recognize and confront our own biases. Education and exposure to diverse perspectives can also broaden awareness of potential biases and promote more inclusive and equitable attitudes and behaviors. Overall, cultivating self-awareness and actively seeking opportunities for introspection and feedback are key strategies for identifying and addressing personal biases. The best leaders who can manage change most effectively are those who are in touch with their own biases, strengths, and weaknesses.

Strategies for Embracing & Navigating Change

The journey of navigating change commences with a fundamental acknowledgment of its existence and a wholehearted acceptance of its presence in our lives. Rather than recoiling from its arrival or attempting to shield ourselves from its effects, we must embrace change as part of the human experience. It is in this acceptance that we unlock the potential for growth and transformation, viewing change not as a disruptor of our stability but as a catalyst for our evolution. By acknowledging and accepting change, we open ourselves to new possibilities, new perspectives, and new opportunities for personal and professional development. This pivotal step sets the foundation for our journey forward, empowering us to navigate the currents of change with resilience, adaptability, and grace.

The Kübler-Ross Change Curve is one of the most widely recognized frameworks used by psychologists to understand and analyze people's behaviors, particularly in response to significant changes or losses. Developed by psychiatrist Elisabeth Kübler-Ross in the context of grief and loss, it has since been adapted and applied to various situations involving change, such as organizational transitions, personal development, and coping with adversity. The stages outlined in the curve provide a valuable framework for understanding the range of emotions and reactions individuals may go through during periods of change, offering insights into how they can navigate and cope with these transitions effectively.

It begins with Shock & Denial, where individuals may resist or deny the need for change, clinging to familiarity. This is followed by Anger, as the reality of change sets in, triggering frustration and resentment towards the situation or those perceived to be responsible. Bargaining comes next, as individuals attempt to negotiate with the change, seeking ways to mitigate its impact or delay its effects. Depression may then set in, characterized by feelings of sadness, loss, and hopelessness as individuals come to terms with the reality of the change. Finally, Acceptance & Integration emerges as individuals begin to embrace the change, finding ways to adapt and move forward constructively, ultimately leading to a sense of resolution and readiness for the new reality.

What's important for leaders to recognize is that people's experiences, genetics and personality traits, and neurology can profoundly influence where they fall on the curve during any given change. For instance, those with a history of successful adaptation may progress through the curve more smoothly, while others may linger in stages of denial or resistance due to fear, uncertainty, or even a neurological predisposition towards risk aversion. Understanding these nuances is essential for leaders orchestrating change initiatives, as it allows for tailored support and interventions to help individuals navigate the transition effectively.

For leaders, it's not uncommon to encounter situations where employees struggle to progress through these stages, or worse, disengage entirely. Ignoring or downplaying these challenges can have detrimental effects, potentially leading to the loss of top talent. Recognizing the signs of resistance or disengagement and addressing them head-on is necessary for fostering a supportive and resilient workforce. By acknowledging employees' struggles, offering support, and facilitating open communication, leaders can help guide them through the change process, ultimately strengthening their resilience and commitment to the organization. Turning a blind eye to these issues only erodes trust and morale, jeopardizing the retention of key talent. With all that said, let's dig into some strategies to embrace and navigate change:

Cultivate Resilience
Resilience is the ability to adapt and bounce back in the face of adversity, trauma, or significant stress. It involves effectively coping with challenges, setbacks, and difficult experiences, while

maintaining a sense of stability and emotional well-being. Resilient people are able to navigate through tough times, learn from setbacks, and emerge stronger and more capable of facing future challenges. Resilience, like a muscle that strengthens with each exertion, is a quality honed through the repetition of life's challenges. It encompasses a multifaceted approach, involving the deliberate cultivation of coping mechanisms, the nurturing of self-care practices, and the wise utilization of support networks comprising friends, family, and mental health professionals. Through deliberate effort and mindful practice, we fortify our resilience, equipping ourselves with the inner strength and emotional fortitude necessary to navigate the change.

In embracing resilience as an essential tool in our arsenal, we not only endure the storms of change but emerge from them with a newfound sense of grace, resilience, and empowerment. As a side note, it's important to remind yourself not to become frustrated with those who haven't experienced what you have—it's not their fault. Everyone's life journey is unique, shaped by different experiences and circumstances. No matter where you are in life, here are several ways to cultivate resilience:

Embrace Self-Care
Commit to self-care practices that nurture your physical, emotional, and mental health, including regular exercise, mindfulness meditation, sufficient sleep, and balanced nutrition. Remember, while discipline is essential in cultivating these habits, it's equally crucial to strive for moderation and balance. Recognize that perfection does not exist and prioritize self-care routines that suit your individual needs and lifestyle.

Maintain Perspective
Foster a positive outlook by viewing setbacks as chances for personal development and advancement. Shift your focus towards aspects within your control rather than fixating on the things you can't control. Knowing what battles to fight and which hills to die on is vital to resilience. It involves discerning between the challenges worth confronting and those better left alone,

allowing yourself to allocate your energy and resources effectively. By choosing wisely, you can preserve your resilience for the battles that truly matter, maximizing your chances of success and well-being in the long run.

Establish Achievable Goals and Productive Habits
Break down ambitious objectives into smaller, achievable tasks, and acknowledge each step of progress. This method not only sustains motivation but also mitigates feelings of being overwhelmed. For those unfamiliar or struggling with this process, *Atomic Habits* by James Clear offers valuable insights and practical strategies to facilitate the development of effective habits. Clear emphasizes the significance of tiny changes or improvements repeated consistently over time, similar to the Japanese philosophy of Kaizen. Both recognize the importance of consistency, persistence, and gradual progress in achieving goals and improving outcomes. They highlight the effectiveness of breaking down larger goals into smaller, more manageable steps, making it easier to sustain motivation and momentum over time.

Embrace Lessons from Adversity
See setbacks as chances for personal development and growth. Reflect on past experiences to extract valuable insights and apply them to future challenges. For instance, I authored this book after experiencing the disappointment of being laid off from an executive position I loved, alongside people I deeply admire. Although difficult, this experience pushed me to step out of my comfort zone and do something new and challenging. It ignited a fire within me to pursue an avenue I hadn't previously considered or even had time for. Instead of allowing adversity to defeat me, I used it as a catalyst for personal and professional growth. In the words of Buddha, "Pain is inevitable, suffering is optional." This shift in perspective propelled me to take a risk, embrace uncertainty, and ultimately, create something meaningful out of a seemingly negative situation. I want the same for you in your next encounter with adversity.

Practice Gratitude

Despite challenges, cultivating gratitude serves as a guiding light through uncertain times, activating brain regions associated with dopamine, linked to pleasure and reward, and stimulating the release of serotonin and oxytocin, fostering happiness and well-being. This practice can lead to long-term changes in neural pathways, promoting mental health and resilience. Therefore, every moment of self-pity becomes a reminder of the privilege to be curious, to create, and to embrace each morning's possibilities with gratitude.

Embrace Support and Connection

In times of change, it's common to feel overwhelmed and anxious. Yet, navigating these transitions does not need to be a solitary endeavor. Seeking support from friends, family, colleagues, and mentors can offer invaluable guidance, encouragement, and perspective. Their practical assistance helps us overcome obstacles and by connecting with others, we not only receive the emotional support vital for navigating change but also cultivate stronger relationships and a sense of community that sustains us through life's challenges. Remember, it's alright to lean on others during these times, often making the journey feel a little less daunting. However, it's crucial to recognize toxic influences and walk away from them if they don't support your success, as they can hinder progress. It may feel like sacrificing everything, but true change often necessitates letting go of what no longer serves your growth. Work to surround yourself with individuals who uplift and empower you.

Focus on a Growth Mindset

The term "growth mindset" first gained prominence with the groundbreaking research conducted by psychologist Carol S. Dweck and her colleagues in the 1990s. Dweck's work, particularly her book "Mindset: The New Psychology of Success," published in 2006, brought the concept to widespread attention. In her research, Dweck explored the idea that individuals' beliefs about their own abilities—whether they believe their intelligence and talents are fixed or can be developed through effort—have profound implications for their motivation, resilience, and success. Since then, the concept of the growth mindset has become a central tenet in the fields of education, psychology, and organizational development, influencing how individuals approach challenges and pursue personal and professional growth. We will break down the many parts of a growth mindset here soon.

Find Humor
Humor truly is the world's best medicine, effortlessly breaking down barriers and fostering connections. Through shared laughter, people find common ground, transcending differences in culture, experience, and perspective. This shared experience creates a sense of camaraderie and establishes an emotional connection that forms the basis of trust and rapport. In tense situations, humor can serve as a powerful tool for diffusing tension, when delivered appropriately. By embracing a lighthearted perspective on life's absurdities, humor fosters empathy and understanding, prompting individuals to see things from different viewpoints and bridging the gap between diverse perspectives. Despite potential cultural or neurological barriers, the universal appeal of humor enables it to transcend boundaries, making navigating change easier as teams bond over shared laughter and find resilience in moments of levity.

In this journey of growth and learning, we need to approach change with an open heart and a willingness to embrace the unknown. We recognize that the path to personal and professional development is not always smooth or linear, but fraught with challenges and setbacks. Yet, it is through these challenges that we discover our true strengths and capabilities, and emerge stronger, wiser, and more resilient than before.

Think back to a moment when you felt stuck or overwhelmed by change. Maybe you were in denial, wishing things would go back to the way they were, or you felt angry and frustrated about the situation.

How did you eventually move past those feelings? What helped you accept and adapt to the new reality?

Consider how you take care of yourself during times of change. What are your go-to strategies for managing stress?

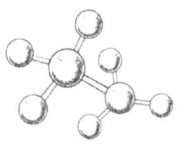

Part 1 Reflection

How might you apply the insights gained from understanding the neuroscience of change and fear in your personal and professional life? What specific strategies or approaches do you intend to implement to navigate resistance and foster a culture of openness and collaboration during times of change?

Reflecting on the Kübler-Ross Change Curve and its stages, how do you identify where you or others might be on the curve during periods of significant change? How can you leverage this understanding to provide tailored support and interventions to help individuals navigate the transition effectively?

Considering the strategies outlined for embracing and navigating change, which ones resonate most with you, and why? How do you envision integrating these strategies into your daily life to cultivate resilience, adaptability, and a growth mindset, both personally and professionally?

PART 2: CULTIVATING A CULTURE OF INNOVATION

Drive Innovation & Embrace Change

In today's fast-paced and rapidly evolving world, innovation has become a key driver of success for organizations across industries. From startups to multinational corporations, fostering a culture of innovation is essential for staying competitive, driving growth, and navigating the challenges of change. In this chapter, we will explore the connection between innovation and change management, discussing techniques for fostering a culture of creativity and experimentation, and highlighting the role of leadership in driving innovation and embracing change.

At its core, innovation is about challenging the status quo, pushing boundaries, and exploring new possibilities. It necessitates a readiness to welcome change, venture into uncertainties, and adjust to new situations. In many ways, innovation and change management are two sides of the same coin - both involve navigating uncertainty, overcoming resistance, and driving transformation.

Think about the uncertainty Thomas Edison must have felt in creating the lightbulb, something we take for granted years later. He attempted thousands of different materials for the filament over almost 10 years of trying before finding success with carbonized bamboo, leading to the invention of the long-lasting, practical incandescent light bulb. And what about a current staple in people's lives – Netflix. Netflix initially started as a DVD rental service but faced serious challenges when the industry shifted towards streaming. The company encountered setbacks such as failed business models, competition from established players, and backlash from customers over pricing changes. However, in the face of failure, Netflix adapted its strategy, invested heavily in original content, and eventually became the dominant force in the streaming industry.

Behind every successful product lies a story of perseverance, resilience, and countless iterations. It's easy to overlook the challenges and setbacks that preceded the final product's success, but they are an integral part of the innovation process. From initial concept to market launch, products undergo rigorous testing, refinement, and adaptation based on feedback and real-world experiences. Each failure, prototype, and setback serve as a learning opportunity, guiding the development process toward eventual success. Recognizing and appreciating the journey of trial and error behind successful products reminds us of the dedication and hard work required to bring innovation to life. Think of it as building product resilience, just like you are building your own resilience. Setbacks and failures are just a natural part of the innovation process, and with perseverance, creativity, and resilience, innovators can overcome these challenges and achieve success.

Most importantly, innovation thrives in environments where change is embraced rather than feared. It requires a culture that values experimentation, creativity, and learning from failure. By incorporating principles of change management into their innovation strategies, organizations can create a fertile ground for new ideas to flourish and evolve.

Building a culture of innovation requires more than just lip service - it requires a deliberate and concerted effort to foster creativity, experimentation, and a willingness to challenge the status quo. This section will provide some techniques for cultivating a culture of innovation.

What is your organization's current approach to innovation?

Are there any existing practices or attitudes that either hinder or support innovation?

Encourage Curiosity and Exploration

Curiosity and exploration are inherent qualities that often flourish during childhood, driven by a natural sense of wonder and an insatiable desire to understand the world. However, as we transition into adulthood, the demands and responsibilities of life can overshadow these intrinsic traits. The pressures to conform to societal expectations, meet obligations, and pursue practical endeavors often result in a gradual suppression of our curiosity and stifling of our inclination to explore. Over time, the pursuit of stability and success can lead us to prioritize practicality over curiosity, pushing imagination to the sidelines as we focus on navigating adulthood. The relentless demands of the world can leave little room for exploration, leaving us feeling trapped in a cycle of routine and obligation.

As a consequence, our once vibrant sense of curiosity becomes subdued, and our capacity for imaginative thinking diminishes. We may find ourselves consumed by the daily grind, struggling to break free from the monotony of routine and reconnect with the sense of wonder that once fueled our curiosity. Yet, despite these challenges, the spark of curiosity remains within us, waiting to be reignited. The greatest leaders are able to embrace moments of reflection, fostering a spirit of open-mindedness and creativity, helping us reclaim our sense of curiosity and reignite our passion for exploration. Through embracing curiosity, we can rediscover the joy of discovery, unlock new perspectives, and cultivate a deeper connection with the world around us.

During change, cultivating a culture that values curiosity and exploration is essential for navigating uncertainties and fostering innovation. As leaders, it's our responsibility to create an environment where curiosity is encouraged, and exploration is embraced. This starts by empowering employees to ask questions, challenge assumptions, and venture into unexplored territories with a sense of curiosity and interest. To do this successfully, you can't be a know-it-all. You must allow space for others to contribute. By instilling a culture of curiosity and exploration, you are empowered to seek out fresh perspectives, discover innovative solutions, and push the boundaries of what's possible. Here are some best practices:

Offer Opportunities for Continuous Learning
Encourage employees to invest in expanding their skills and knowledge through workshops, seminars, and training programs. This not only fosters personal growth but also creates opportunities for meaningful conversation and critical thinking that can spawn new ideas.

Foster a Safe Space for Thinking
Some companies have think-tank room, encourage their employees to go for thinking walks, or provide dedicated spaces for creative brainstorming and problem-solving. These environments are designed to foster innovation by allowing people to step away from their regular workstations and immerse themselves in a different setting that stimulates fresh ideas. Whether it's a designated room equipped with tools for visualization and collaboration or simply a stroll outdoors, these practices encourage employees to break free from routine thinking patterns, engage in deep reflection, and generate innovative solutions to complex challenges.

Unlock the Full Potential of Your Teams
Promoting curiosity and exploration ignites employees' passion for discovery and drives them towards excellence. By providing opportunities for skill development and cross-functional collaboration, organizations enable individuals to leverage their full potential and achieve collective success. For example, setting up job shares or job rotations can spark new conversations with different people by facilitating cross-functional collaboration and knowledge sharing. Job shares allow employees to work closely with a partner, exchanging ideas and perspectives while jointly tackling responsibilities. These practices not only broaden employees' skill sets and experiences but also foster a culture of

collaboration and innovation as individuals bring fresh insights and approaches from their interactions with others.

Embrace the Journey of Discovery Together
When a company actively promotes and supports curiosity and exploration as fundamental values within its culture, it fosters ongoing learning and discovery among its teams. By organizing sessions where knowledge is shared and encouraging collaborations across different disciplines, organizations cultivate an environment where innovation and adaptability thrive. By collectively embracing the process of exploration and discovery, teams are better equipped to overcome challenges and capitalize on opportunities for progress and advancement.

How would you describe the culture surrounding creativity, experimentation, and risk-taking?

How can you cultivate a culture that not only tolerates but actively encourages risk-taking and curiosity in the workplace, ultimately fostering innovation and growth while still holding people accountable?

Embrace Diversity and Inclusion

In today's interconnected world, diversity isn't just a buzzword – it's a fundamental cornerstone of success. As leaders, it's incumbent upon us to cultivate environments where diversity of thought, background, and perspective flourish. A prior leader of mine confidently claimed that Diversity, Equity, and Inclusion (DEI) efforts were unnecessary because our company supposedly "didn't face any DEI issues." However, his surprise and dismay were palpable when the results of the employee survey revealed a different reality. Confronted with data contradicting his beliefs, he responded poorly to proposals for implementing DEI programs within the company. Despite employees' awareness of the need for change, the decision not to invest in DEI initiatives came from the top, despite clear indications from the data that such investment was necessary.

This type of attitude completely undermines the importance of proactive DEI initiatives in fostering inclusive workplaces where every voice is valued and respected because encouraging diversity isn't just about ticking boxes or meeting quotas; it's about acknowledging the invaluable contributions that diverse perspectives offer. In addition, DEI extends beyond race alone, a misconception some still hold. It encompasses diverse perspectives such as neurodiversity, socioeconomics, gender, alongside many others. Discussing this isn't about seeking special treatment either but rather about demonstrating empathy and compassion, and fostering an environment where everyone can thrive.

Furthermore, labeling DEI advocates as "special snowflakes" or DEI initiatives as "woke" only reveals a person's unwillingness to look beyond what is comfortable for them. Resorting to derogatory labels undermines the important work of fostering inclusive and equitable spaces, while perpetuating harmful stereotypes and attitudes. To effectively address diversity and inclusion, it's imperative to cultivate an environment of respectful dialogue and understanding. By fostering a culture that values and celebrates differences, we tap into a source of creativity and innovation that propels our organizations forward. When people from varied backgrounds come together, they bring with them a wealth of experiences, insights, and ideas that can spark groundbreaking innovations and solutions.

Furthermore, championing inclusion goes hand in hand with embracing diversity. It's not enough to simply have diverse voices in the room – we must ensure that all voices are heard, respected, and valued. Inclusive practices create an environment where everyone feels welcome and empowered to contribute their unique perspectives. By fostering a culture of inclusivity, we not only enhance employee morale and engagement but also unlock the full potential of our teams, driving collaboration, productivity, and ultimately, success. If you find yourself disregarding or not wanting to hear certain voices, it may be a sign that you're hiring the wrong people, or not fostering an inclusive environment where all perspectives are valued.

According to a McKinsey & Company report, companies in the top quartile for racial and ethnic diversity are 35% more likely to have financial returns above their respective national industry medians, a statistic that is more than psychology-based evidence. By embracing diversity and inclusion, these organizations harness the unique perspectives and talents of their diverse workforce, leading to greater innovation, creativity, and overall performance.

And much like my prior boss, it's not uncommon to encounter individuals who harbor fear or apprehension towards diversity. Some CEOs and leaders may be hesitant to implement DEI programs in their workplaces for various reasons. Here are a few possible explanations:

Lack of Understanding
Some leaders may not fully grasp the importance and benefits of DEI initiatives. They might view such programs as unnecessary or irrelevant to their organization's goals and success.

Fear of Change
Implementing DEI programs often requires significant organizational change and may challenge existing power dynamics. Some leaders may fear disruption or resistance from employees accustomed to the status quo.

Perceived Threat to Status
In hierarchical organizations, leaders may feel threatened by initiatives that aim to level the playing field or promote diversity. They may worry that DEI efforts will diminish their authority or privilege.

Concerns About Backlash
Introducing DEI programs can sometimes provoke backlash from certain employees or stakeholders who perceive them as preferential treatment or "political correctness gone mad." Leaders may hesitate to navigate these potential conflicts.

Lack of Resources
DEI initiatives often require dedicated time, effort, and resources to implement effectively. Some leaders may focus on other business priorities or feel unable to allocate resources to DEI programs.

Misguided Beliefs
Unfortunately, some leaders may hold biased or discriminatory beliefs that lead them to oppose DEI efforts. They may downplay the importance of diversity or believe in meritocracy without recognizing systemic barriers to equal opportunity.

If you notice any of these, you may find that you need to manage up with resistance to DEI initiatives, and this requires a strategic approach aimed at addressing leaders' concerns and fostering a greater understanding of the importance of DEI. Here are some tactics that may help:

Educate and Advocate
Provide leaders with data, research, and case studies demonstrating the business benefits of DEI initiatives, such as improved innovation, employee engagement, and financial performance. Help them understand that diversity is not just a moral imperative but also a strategic advantage.

Frame DEI as a Business Imperative
Speak to their ethos. Emphasize how DEI initiatives align with the organization's mission, values, and long-term goals. Position diversity as a driver of innovation, creativity, and competitiveness in today's diverse marketplace.

Highlight Success Stories
Share success stories from other organizations that have implemented effective DEI programs. Showcase concrete examples of how diversity initiatives have positively impacted employee morale, productivity, and bottom-line results.

Address Concerns Proactively
Take the time to listen to leaders' concerns and address them proactively. Be prepared to provide evidence-based responses to common objections, such as fears of preferential treatment or concerns about backlash.

Build Coalitions of Support
Identify allies within the organization who can help advocate for DEI initiatives. Engage with influential stakeholders, including senior leaders, HR professionals, and employee resource groups, to build support for diversity efforts.

Offer Solutions, Not Just Problems
Instead of simply highlighting issues or disparities, present concrete solutions, and actionable steps for addressing them. Focus on practical measures that leaders can implement to promote diversity and inclusion within their teams and departments.

Lead by Example
Demonstrate your commitment to diversity and inclusion through your own actions and behaviors. Champion DEI initiatives within your sphere of influence and serve as a role model for others to follow. If you're not in a position to lead these initiatives, you can still be an ally. You can demonstrate your commitment to diversity and inclusion through your own actions and behaviors.

Be Patient and Persistent
Changing attitudes and behaviors takes time, so be patient and persistent in your efforts. Stay focused on the long-term benefits of diversity and continue to advocate for positive change.

By employing these strategies, you can begin to approach potential resistance to DEI initiatives and help drive meaningful progress towards a more diverse, equitable, and inclusive workplace that is ready to change as the rest of the world changes.

Consider the state of DEI within your organization. Reflect on the extent to which DEI principles are integrated into company policies, practices, and culture.

How does your organization currently address issues of diversity, equity, and inclusion, and what areas might need improvement or further attention?

Promote Collaboration and Cross-Pollination

In the fast-paced landscape of modern organizations, the siloed approach to work is quickly becoming obsolete. To remain agile and innovative, organizational leaders must break down these barriers and foster collaboration across teams and departments. This involves creating a culture that not only values collaboration but actively promotes it as a means of driving growth and creativity.

Encouraging collaboration entails fostering a culture that prioritizes the seamless exchange of ideas, resources, and expertise among team members. It's not just about assembling teams for projects; rather, it involves nurturing a mindset where sharing is ingrained. Through initiatives like cross-functional teams, brainstorming sessions, and knowledge-sharing platforms, organizations can facilitate the flow of insights and perspectives that drive innovation. However, failing to embrace this thinking can lead to the default practice of hoarding information, either by individuals or teams, which poses significant risks.

Hoarding information, whether at an individual or team level, erects barriers to effective collaboration and hampers organizational progress. While information hoarders may feel they are protecting their jobs, it really just fosters a culture of isolation and mistrust among colleagues, hindering collective success. When teams, or individuals, hoard information, they limit their ability to leverage diverse perspectives and expertise, stifling creativity and problem-solving. This behavior not only obstructs innovation but also undermines team cohesion and organizational agility. Therefore, promoting transparency and open communication is crucial to mitigating the dangers associated with information hoarding, fostering a collaborative environment conducive to sustained growth and success.

When information flows freely and communication channels remain unobstructed, teams can work more efficiently and make better-informed decisions. This culture of transparency builds trust among employees and fosters a sense of collective ownership over the organization's goals and objectives.

Indeed, it's a reality that you might find yourself leading a team where certain employees simply don't play well with others, resulting in some challenges. When this happens, here are a few strategies that may help:

Establish clear goals and expectations: Clearly define the team's objectives and the role each member plays in achieving them. When everyone understands the common purpose, they are more likely to set aside personal differences and focus on the shared goal. This not only fosters a collaborative atmosphere but also decreases the chances of people inadvertently stepping on each other's toes, as mutual respect and alignment reduce conflicts and misunderstandings.

Promote collaboration through team-building activities: Organize team-building activities and workshops that promote collaboration and strengthen interpersonal relationships. These activities can help break down barriers and build trust among team members. And even though people may not initially love the idea of team building, when done well, it often ends up being enjoyable and beneficial, effectively fulfilling its intended purpose. Team-building activities can break down barriers and build trust among team members, ultimately strengthening interpersonal relationships.

Assign complementary roles: Recognize each team member's strengths and weaknesses and assign roles that complement their skills. By leveraging each member's strengths, you can create a more balanced and cohesive team. The Clifton StrengthsFinder is a powerful tool for understanding individual strengths within a team. By assessing natural talents and inclinations, this assessment and book provides valuable insights into each team member's unique abilities. These insights can inform role assignments and task delegation, maximizing productivity and job satisfaction. Additionally, StrengthsFinder fosters better communication and collaboration by promoting diverse strengths. Ultimately, leveraging a tool like this will help in assigning complimentary roles and can lead to a more effective team dynamic, driving overall success and achievement of organizational goals.

Mediate conflicts: It's remarkable how many leaders shy away from conflict resolution. However, avoiding conflict can have detrimental effects because it allows underlying issues to fester and escalate, potentially leading to resentment, decreased morale, and decreased productivity among team members. Moreover, unresolved conflicts can erode trust and collaboration within the team, hindering progress and innovation. Effective leaders recognize the importance of addressing conflicts head-on, fostering open communication, and promoting a culture of respect and accountability within the team no matter how uncomfortable. By addressing conflicts constructively, leaders can strengthen relationships, promote growth, and drive positive outcomes for the organization as a whole. If you lack the inclination to address conflicts, perhaps pursuing a leadership role isn't the best fit for you, and that's perfectly okay. If you choose to pursue it, be prepared to challenge yourself actively and push beyond your comfort zone.

Lead by example: Demonstrate collaborative behavior as a leader by actively engaging with team members, soliciting their input, and valuing their contributions. Your actions will set the tone for the team and encourage collaborative behavior among members.

By implementing these strategies, leaders can create an environment where team members are motivated to join forces, despite differences in personalities or interpersonal dynamics.

Promoting cross-pollination of ideas further enhances collaboration by encouraging individuals to step outside their comfort zones and engage with colleagues from diverse backgrounds and expertise areas. By breaking down the barriers between departments, you can create an environment where fresh perspectives can converge, leading to breakthrough innovations and novel solutions to complex challenges. This camaraderie is particularly valuable given the considerable amount of time we spend together at work, often surpassing any other context in our lives.

Reflect on the collaborative landscape within your organization. Consider the current level of collaboration and cross-pollination among teams, departments, and individuals.

How effectively does your organization promote collaboration, knowledge sharing, and interdisciplinary cooperation?

Are there existing practices or barriers that hinder or facilitate collaboration, and what opportunities exist for enhancing cross-functional interaction and innovation?

Provide Resources and Support

Innovation is fueled by resources, both tangible and intangible, and organizations must prioritize providing employees with the necessary tools, training, and support to foster innovation and experimentation. It's essential to recognize that employees may not inherently possess all the skills or knowledge required for every task or project they're assigned. Making assumptions about their capabilities can lead to frustration, disengagement, and ultimately hinder productivity. How often do we encounter the sentiment, "I hired them specifically for this task, yet I'm frustrated by their inability to perform it"? This frustration often stems from a misalignment between expectations and reality, highlighting the importance of clear communication, ongoing feedback, and perhaps reevaluation of roles and responsibilities. By providing comprehensive training, access to necessary tools, and ample resources, leaders can empower their teams to perform at their best.

This might include training programs, mentorship opportunities, or access to online platforms like Coursera, Udemy, and LinkedIn Learning. Virtual conferences and networking events also offer affordable learning opportunities, enabling individuals to participate without the added expense of travel. By prioritizing and investing in employees' learning and development initiatives, leaders not only demonstrate their commitment to nurturing their workforce but also significantly enhance their ability to retain top talent and elevate overall morale within the organization. According to LinkedIn's 2019 Workplace Learning Report, a remarkable 94% of employees indicate that they would be inclined to stay with a company for a longer period if such investments were made.

This also includes onboarding programs for new hires, as this is when we set the tone for all new employees. When you go to lead a change initiative, this part of the employee lifecycle is paramount since first impressions set the stage for future interactions and relationships. The initial encounters that employees have with their colleagues, managers, and the overall organizational environment can shape their perceptions and experiences throughout their tenure. Positive first impressions can foster trust, rapport, and goodwill, facilitating effective communication and collaboration. Conversely, negative first impressions may create barriers to building relationships and can lead to misunderstandings or conflict. Additionally, how individuals present themselves in terms of appearance, demeanor, and communication style can influence perceptions of competence, professionalism, and credibility, impacting their professional reputation within the organization. Therefore, cultivating positive first impressions is essential for establishing productive, and mutually beneficial relationships in the workplace.

Consider the following best practices for an onboarding program. As you review these, reflect on your organization's current practices, and identify areas for improvement. Which components are already implemented, and how can they be enhanced to better support new employees' integration and success within the organization?

- Clearly outlined roles, responsibilities, and performance expectations for new employees from the outset. This sets the foundation for success and helps align individual goals with organizational objectives.

- A thorough orientation to the company, including its history, culture, values, and mission. This helps newcomers understand the organization's identity and fosters a sense of belonging from the start.

- Structured training programs tailored to the specific needs of each role. This may include technical skills training, job shadowing opportunities, mentorship programs, and access to online learning resources.

- New employees paired with seasoned colleagues who can serve as a mentor or buddy during the onboarding process. This provides additional support, guidance, and a source of informal knowledge transfer.

- Scheduled regular check-in meetings between new hires and their managers to assess progress, provide feedback, and address any questions or concerns. This helps new employees feel supported and ensures they are on track to meet performance expectations.

- Opportunities for new employees to get to know their colleagues and build relationships across the organization. This may include team-building activities, social events, and networking opportunities.

- Access to the tools, resources, and support they need to succeed in their roles. This may include technology, software systems, HR support, and access to relevant documentation or policies.

- Regularly review and evaluate the effectiveness of the onboarding program to identify areas for improvement. Solicit feedback from new hires to understand their experience and adjust as needed to enhance the onboarding process over time.

Additionally, offering access to relevant tools and resources to all employees is necessary for high engagement and productivity. This might involve providing software programs, equipment, or access to industry publications and research materials. Tangible resources such as access to the appropriate technology, research facilities, and financial backing can empower employees to explore new ideas and turn them into reality. In instances where the organization's budget cannot meet its needs, honesty becomes crucial.

Alongside exploring alternative technology solutions, it's important for companies to honestly reassess the workload they're expecting from their employees. This involves critically evaluating project requirements and objectives to determine if there are any tasks or deliverables that could be streamlined, simplified, or reprioritized to reduce the need for extensive technology resources. By openly communicating with employees about workload expectations and exploring opportunities to optimize project scope and workflow efficiency, companies can mitigate the strain on limited technology resources while still achieving project goals effectively. This approach not only helps address immediate budget constraints but also fosters a collaborative and supportive work environment that prioritizes employee well-being and productivity. While I am not blind to the fact that there may be decision-makers and stakeholders unaware of the ground-floor realities, it remains a necessity for senior leaders to attentively listen to the needs of the company and reallocate resourcing when possible.

Equally important are intangible resources like mentorship, guidance, and a supportive organizational culture that encourages risk-taking and learning for all employees, not just new ones. Investing in dedicated spaces to learn and share ideas can provide employees with the physical infrastructure needed to collaborate, experiment, and test new concepts. These spaces serve as creative hubs where individuals from diverse backgrounds and expertise areas can come together to brainstorm ideas, prototype solutions, and iterate on their discoveries. By creating a conducive environment for innovation, organizations signal their commitment to fostering creativity and supporting employees' entrepreneurial endeavors.

By investing in continuous learning initiatives, organizations empower employees to stay ahead of emerging trends, acquire new skills, and explore new approaches to problem-solving. Providing access to mentors, subject matter experts, and external networks can also facilitate knowledge sharing and collaboration, enabling employees to tap into a wealth of expertise and insights. Organizations that invest in both tangible resources and intangible support demonstrate their dedication to fostering innovation, positioning themselves as industry leaders.

Sadly, the field of training and development is often overlooked or the last to be funded, much like the arts in educational settings, despite its potential significance for brain development and growth. While it may be seen as expendable initially, it holds the potential to profoundly impact the human brain's growth and cognitive abilities. Not only that but according to the most recent LinkedIn Workplace Learning Report, nearly 70% of employees view training and development opportunities provided by their companies as vital for their job satisfaction. Prioritizing resources and support for innovation within organizations is not just beneficial but essential for a company's success.

Consider the level of resources and support available within your organization for fostering innovation and creativity. Reflect on the existing infrastructure, programs, and initiatives designed to support employees in their innovative endeavors.

Are there dedicated channels or platforms for sharing ideas and collaborating across teams?

How accessible are resources such as training programs, mentorship opportunities, and funding for innovative projects?

Build Psychological Safety

When you encourage curiosity and exploration, embrace diversity and inclusion, promote collaboration and cross-pollination, reward risk-taking, and provide resources and support, you are helping to build psychological safety which is critical for innovation and adaptability.

The term "psychological safety" was coined by Amy Edmondson in the early 1990s. Edmondson conducted extensive research on team dynamics and organizational behavior, particularly in the context of healthcare settings. She first introduced the concept in her landmark paper titled "Psychological Safety and Learning Behavior in Work Teams," published in the Administrative Science Quarterly journal in 1999. Since then, psychological safety has gained widespread recognition and has been studied and applied in various organizational contexts beyond healthcare, including business, education, and technology. Piggybacking on Edmondson's work, Google conducted a comprehensive study known as "Project Aristotle" to understand what makes teams effective. Google found that teams with higher levels of psychological safety were more likely to be successful and innovative, more so than any other factor, including dependability, structure, clarity, meaning, and impact.

In an effort to make this concept more tangible, consider it from a physical safety perspective. Imagine yourself bungee jumping: perched atop a towering 500-foot platform, your heart races with anticipation, and doubts cloud your mind about the decision you've made. As you summon the courage to move closer to the edge, you overhear the jump operator joking around with his partner, sparking uncertainty within you. Thoughts flood your mind: Are they not taking this seriously? What if they didn't secure me correctly? How many accidents have happened? Why did I choose to do this? You sense being left alone to your own devices. Are they professionals or complacent? The pivotal question remains: Do you take the leap? Feeling physically safe resonates deeply because it's tangible—we can see it, touch it, even hear it. Psychological safety operates similarly. It triggers the same reactions as the bungee scenario, but we often can't outwardly express it—we just *feel* it. Consequently, psychological safety stems from a neurological response and:

Encourages Open Communication

When team members feel psychologically safe, they are more likely to communicate openly and honestly. This open communication fosters trust and transparency within the team, enabling leaders to gather diverse perspectives, ideas, and feedback essential for making informed decisions and driving successful change initiatives.

Fosters Innovation and Creativity

Psychological safety creates an environment where individuals feel empowered to share innovative ideas and take calculated risks without the fear of embarrassment or ridicule. This freedom to experiment and explore drives an organization's ability to adapt and thrive in an ever-changing environment.

Supports Learning and Development

In psychologically safe environments, individuals are more willing to seek feedback, ask questions, and engage in continuous learning and development. They feel comfortable admitting mistakes and weaknesses, knowing that they won't be judged or penalized. This openness to learning promotes personal and professional growth, enabling leaders and team members to develop new skills and capabilities necessary for navigating change successfully.

Builds Resilience

Psychological safety contributes to building resilience within teams and organizations. When individuals feel supported and valued, they are better equipped to cope with challenges, setbacks, and uncertainties associated with change. They are more likely to bounce back from defeat, adapt to new circumstances, and remain committed to achieving shared goals, contributing to the overall resilience of the organization.

There are people who dismiss psychological safety as merely a buzzword, question its necessity in driving organizational success, and will potentially even mock the concept. Either they haven't been bungee jumping, or these factors may be in play:

A lack of awareness: They may not fully understand the concept of psychological safety or its significance in fostering a healthy and productive work environment. They may be unfamiliar with the extensive research that demonstrates the positive impact of psychological safety on team performance and innovation.

Misguided beliefs: There may be misconceptions or misunderstandings about what psychological safety entails. Some individuals may mistakenly equate psychological safety with coddling or excessive sensitivity, rather than recognizing it as a fundamental aspect of creating an inclusive and supportive workplace culture. These people may just push their friend off the bungee platform.

Cultural norms: In certain organizational cultures or industries, there may be a prevailing mindset that prioritizes toughness, competition, and individual achievement over collaboration and emotional well-being. In such environments, psychological safety may be undervalued or even seen as a sign of weakness.

Fear of vulnerability: For some individuals, the idea of creating an environment where people feel comfortable expressing their thoughts, opinions, and concerns may be uncomfortable or intimidating. They may fear that encouraging openness and vulnerability will lead to conflict or undermine authority.

Prior negative experiences: Individuals who have experienced betrayal, ridicule, or punishment in response to sharing their ideas or concerns in the past may be hesitant to believe in the importance of psychological safety. Past negative experiences can shape perceptions and attitudes towards interpersonal trust and risk-taking.

Addressing barriers to innovation requires education, dialogue, and a commitment to fostering a culture of inclusivity. Psychological safety is pivotal for effective leadership and change management, enabling individuals to express themselves and innovate without fear of repercussion. Encouraging collaboration, providing resources for growth, and embracing both successes and failures are vital for nurturing an innovative culture, where continuous learning and improvement thrive under the guidance of organizational leaders.

Do team members feel empowered to take risks and explore new approaches, knowing that they have the support and trust of their colleagues and leaders?

Are there established channels for providing feedback and addressing conflicts in a constructive and respectful manner?

How do leaders model and promote psychological safety within their teams and across your organization?

Part 2 Reflection

Reflecting on your organization's current approach to fostering innovation, which techniques for promoting a culture of creativity and experimentation do you believe could be most effectively implemented, and why?

How might you integrate principles of DEI into your organization's innovation strategy to ensure that a wide range of perspectives and experiences are represented in the ideation and decision-making processes?

Considering the importance of psychological safety in fostering innovation and risk-taking, what specific actions can you take as a leader to create an environment where team members feel empowered to take creative risks and learn from failure without fear of judgment or reprisal?

PART 3: THE ROLE OF LEADERSHIP IN DRIVING INNOVATION AND EMBRACING CHANGE

Lead by Example

Leadership plays a most crucial role in driving innovation and fostering a culture of change within organizations. As I touched on previously, fostering a culture of innovation leads to tangible business benefits. Deloitte researchers found that organizations with a strong innovation culture are 3.5 times more likely to outperform their peers in revenue growth over a five-year period. But it doesn't happen on its own. Leaders must set the tone, establish the vision, and create the conditions for innovation to thrive.

To lead by example effectively, leaders must demonstrate a willingness to embrace change and take risks. They should be visible champions of innovation, encouraging experimentation, and celebrating success, fostering a culture of openness and transparency, where ideas are welcomed, and yes, where failures are seen as learning opportunities. By leading with authenticity and vulnerability, leaders inspire trust and create a sense of psychological safety where employees feel empowered to take risks and innovate without fear of judgment or consequence.

Furthermore, leaders should prioritize communication and collaboration, actively engage with their teams to share their vision, solicit feedback, and align everyone towards common goals. This encourages a culture of accountability and ownership, where everyone feels invested in the organization's success and motivated to contribute their best efforts.

In addition to leading by example in their professional lives, leaders should also prioritize self-care and work-life balance. When leaders work excessively long hours, their team may perceive this as the expected norm, potentially leading to burnout and resentment among employees. Moreover, when leaders openly complain about their workload or constantly emphasize how busy they are, it sets a tone that suggests overwork is commendable or necessary for success. However, when leaders prioritize their own well-being by occasionally taking vacations or mental health days to spend with family or friends, it humanizes them and fosters a sense of connection and safety within the team. By prioritizing physical and mental health, leaders set a positive example for their team and cultivate a culture that values holistic well-being, ultimately contributing to a more productive, engaged, and fulfilled workforce.

An analogy that may resonate with some is that leading by example at work is really no different than parenting at home. Just as parents set the tone for their children by modeling behaviors they wish to instill, leaders influence their teams through their actions and attitudes. Much like how children observe and emulate their parents' conduct, employees observe their leaders' behavior and follow suit. Just because people grow up and become adults, it doesn't change this fundamental aspect of human nature. When parents exhibit patience, kindness, and resilience, children learn to embody these qualities.

In the workplace, when leaders resort to raising their voices and placing blame, the repercussions are far-reaching. Such behavior instills fear and intimidation, creating a hostile environment that stifles creativity and collaboration. Individuals may feel pressured to prioritize self-preservation over honesty, leading to a pattern of lying as a coping mechanism in response to perceived threats or conflicts. Their response to yelling or blaming is not indicative of weakness or lack of toughness though.

Rather, it reflects the profound impact of stress and negative environments on neurological processes. Yelling or blaming triggers the amygdala, heightening emotions like fear and anxiety, and activating the body's fight-or-flight response. It also triggers the prefrontal cortex, responsible for executive functions such as decision-making and impulse control, to become less active. This can impair individuals' ability to think rationally and make sound judgments, making them more susceptible to impulsive behavior, such as lying, as a means of self-preservation. As you can imagine, this negatively impacts creativity, innovation, and collaboration. Blame creates a culture of distrust and low morale, fostering resentment and disengagement within the team. This negative atmosphere often leads to increased turnover rates.

Chronic stress further compounds these effects, impacting brain structure and function, and it perpetuates the cycle of fear and dishonesty in the workplace. Chronic exposure to stressful or hostile environments can actually lead to changes in brain structure and function over time. For example, prolonged stress can impair the functioning of the hippocampus, a brain region involved in memory and emotion regulation, potentially affecting individuals' ability to recall accurate information or regulate their emotions effectively.

Furthermore, social and environmental factors play a significant role in shaping behavior. If individuals perceive yelling or blaming as a regular occurrence in their environment, they may learn to associate honesty with negative consequences and dishonesty with self-preservation. It's no surprise then that children, particularly teenagers, resort to lying frequently as they prioritize self-preservation. When this behavior isn't addressed adequately, it can persist into adulthood. Over time, this learned tendency becomes reinforced, creating a pattern of lying as a coping mechanism in the face of perceived threats or conflicts.

Additionally, leaders who lead with anger and blame set a poor example and promote a culture of defensiveness rather than accountability and problem-solving. This behavior undermines the leader's credibility and authority, damages relationships, and overall organizational performance. Conversely, when leaders demonstrate calmness, adaptability, integrity, and a growth mindset, their team members are inspired to do the same. Thus, whether in the office or at home, leading by example is not just a strategy but a way of life that fosters growth, development, and positive outcomes. Leading by example requires leaders to embody the values and behaviors they wish to see in their teams and organizations. It involves treating others how you want to be treated. Period.

Think of a situation where a leader effectively modeled behavior for their team, setting a clear example of the values and expectations they wished to instill within the organization. What specific actions or behaviors stood out in that situation?

What obstacles do you encounter that hinder your ability to lead by example?

Can leaders truly cultivate a culture of trust, respect, and collaboration if they do not lead by example?

Empower and Support Employees

Empowering employees entails granting them the authority, autonomy, resources, and support required to make decisions, take initiative, and contribute meaningfully to the organization's goals. It involves fostering a work environment where individuals feel valued, respected, and confident in their abilities to innovate, problem-solve, and drive positive change. As a result, research shows that organizations with high levels of employee engagement and empowerment outperform their competitors in key metrics like profitability and productivity.

Leaders can cultivate such empowerment by fostering a culture that values contributions from all levels, encouraging employees to share their ideas, insights, and expertise. Creating avenues for individuals to share ideas, tackle fresh challenges, and explore novel approaches via specialized platforms for brainstorming and teamwork is vital for nurturing an environment of empowerment and creativity. In order to get there though, you'll have to ask questions like these to recognize what your employees want and need to feel empowered:

- What do you need to succeed in your role?

- How can I support you in achieving your goals?

- What opportunities for growth and development are you interested in pursuing?

- What challenges are you facing, and how can we overcome them together?

- What ideas or suggestions do you have for improving our processes or operations?

- How do you prefer to receive feedback, and how can I provide support in your professional development?

- What strengths and skills do you bring to the team, and how can we leverage them effectively?

- What projects or tasks are you passionate about, and how can we align your interests with our organizational objectives?

- How can we create a work environment that allows you to thrive and feel valued?

- What autonomy or decision-making authority would enable you to make a greater impact in your role?

These questions demonstrate a commitment to empowering employees by soliciting their input, valuing their perspectives, and providing support tailored to their individual needs and aspirations. But it's also essential to create a concrete plan to execute these ideas with your employees, demonstrating a genuine commitment to employee empowerment and growth. Without follow-through, employees may perceive these inquiries as mere lip service, eroding trust and diminishing morale not just with you but within the organization.

This approach stands in stark contrast to micromanagement, where there is excessive control, close supervision, and involvement in every aspect of employees' work, and evaluating whether you are a micromanager is crucial for fostering a positive work environment and promoting employee engagement and growth. Micromanagement can have detrimental effects on morale, hindering productivity and stifling innovation. And as we know, awareness and a willingness to adapt management styles contribute to personal growth and development, leading to more effective and fulfilling leadership practices. Therefore, I will challenge you to evaluate your micromanagement tendencies.

Here are some questions you can ask yourself to assess if you might be micromanaging:

- Do I find myself constantly checking in on my employees' progress and tasks?

- Am I reluctant to delegate tasks or responsibilities because I believe I can do them better myself?

- Do I provide detailed instructions on how tasks should be completed, without allowing room for creativity or innovation?

- Do I frequently intervene or "take over" when I perceive things aren't being done the way I want them to be?

- Do I have difficulty trusting my team members to work independently and make decisions without my input?

- Am I overly concerned with minor details and insist on being involved in every decision, no matter how small?

- Do I frequently second-guess or criticize my employees' work, even when it meets expectations?

- Do I tend to micromanage certain individuals or projects more than others?

- Do I prioritize control and oversight over empowering and developing my team members?

- Do I feel stressed or overwhelmed by the amount of work I need to oversee, leading me to micromanage out of fear of failure or incompetence?

Reflecting on these questions can help you recognize if you might be exhibiting micromanagement tendencies and identify areas for improvement in your management approach. There are instances when resorting to micromanagement is necessary, such as during times of crisis or when working on critical projects with tight deadlines. However, it's important to recognize that micromanagement should be the exception rather than the rule.

Empowering and supporting employees are integral components of fostering psychological safety within an organization, especially during times of change. When employees feel empowered, they are more likely to speak up, share their ideas, and take risks without fear of retribution. When employees are micromanaged, they feel disempowered, demotivated, and disengaged. If leaders are hesitant to trust their employees enough to empower them, it may be necessary to critically evaluate hiring practices and examine how leadership is establishing the organizational tone, fostering an environment of mutual trust and collaboration conducive to successful change management.

Reflect on a time when you felt empowered in your role to contribute ideas and take on new challenges. How did this experience impact your motivation and engagement at work?

How good is your company at building a culture of continuous learning and development?

What specific strategies or initiatives do they have to support employees' growth and empower them to innovate?

Remove Barriers and Roadblocks

Effective leaders understand the importance of identifying and eliminating barriers and roadblocks that impede innovation and change within the organization. They recognize that such obstacles can hinder progress and stifle creativity, preventing the organization from realizing its full potential.

One approach to removing barriers is to break down silos we mentioned earlier and foster collaboration across departments and teams. Silos often create communication bottlenecks and inhibit the flow of ideas and information. Encouraging cross-functional collaboration and fostering teamwork towards shared objectives enables leaders to dismantle silos and cultivate an open, collaborative culture. Achieving this requires leaders forming and building on those partnerships with fellow leaders across the organization.

As maybe you have, I've witnessed instances where even senior leaders fail to communicate with one another, leading to a lack of cross-team collaboration entirely. The consequence of inadequate communication and collaboration among top leaders frequently manifests in the dysfunctionality of their respective teams. When leaders fail to engage in cross-functional dialogue and cooperation, it leads to siloed working environments where teams operate in isolation, hindering productivity, innovation, and overall organizational performance. This fragmentation can result in duplicated efforts, missed opportunities for synergy, and a disjointed approach to problem-solving. Ultimately, it undermines the organization's ability to adapt to change, meet strategic objectives, and thrive in a competitive marketplace.

Additionally, leaders should streamline processes and eliminate unnecessary bureaucracy that can slow down innovation efforts. In my experience, I witnessed the attempt to roll out a PMO to a company that had never had one before. However, the approach was overly technical and complicated, far beyond what the organization needed. The lack of user-friendliness and over-engineering led to widespread reluctance and disengagement among employees. It was too complex and rigid and became a barrier rather than a benefit. The masses became stuck in the Desire phase of the Kübler-Ross Change Curve, reluctant to move further. When we re-introduced it into the organization in small, manageable increments rather than over-engineering it, we experienced greater buy-in and success. The refined approach allowed employees to gradually acclimate to the new processes and tools, with more communication and training, fostering a greater sense of ownership and participation in the implementation process.

By breaking down the initiative into smaller, more digestible components, we were able to address specific needs and concerns more effectively, leading to increased engagement and adoption across the organization. This highlights the significance of adopting a strategic and iterative change management approach, emphasizing practical solutions that resonate with the organization's culture and capacities. Attempting to force a square peg into a round hole is pointless and counterproductive. However, several tools can help streamline processes and manage roadblocks effectively during change initiatives. Here are some examples:

Project Management Software
Utilizing project management software such as Smartsheet, Asana, Trello, or Jira can help teams organize tasks, track progress, and collaborate more efficiently. These tools provide visibility into project timelines, assign responsibilities, and facilitate communication. Understand the readiness of your organization. For instance, we initially referred to our PMO as the Fisher Price PMO and began with Trello, later transitioning to Smartsheets, which proved effective for us. However, your organization might be ready to start with something more complex from the outset.

Process Mapping Tools
Process mapping tools like Lucidchart or Microsoft Visio enable teams to visually map out existing processes, identify bottlenecks, and streamline workflows. By visualizing processes, teams can better understand the flow of work and identify opportunities for improvement.

Change Management Software
Change management software, such as Prosci or ChangeScout, helps organizations plan, track, and manage change initiatives effectively. These tools provide frameworks for assessing change readiness, developing communication plans, and monitoring the impact of change on stakeholders.

Collaboration Platforms
Collaboration tools such as Slack, Microsoft Teams, or Google Workspace enable seamless communication and teamwork in real-time, regardless of team members' geographical locations. These platforms enable teams to share documents, hold virtual meetings, and collaborate on projects more seamlessly.

Lean Six Sigma Methodology
Implementing Lean Six Sigma methodologies can help organizations identify and eliminate waste, reduce variation, and improve process efficiency. Tools like value stream mapping, root cause analysis, and DMAIC (Define, Measure, Analyze, Improve, Control) can be used to streamline processes and address roadblocks effectively.

Continuous Improvement Tools
Tools such as Kaizen, Gemba walks, and quality circles promote a culture of continuous improvement within organizations. These tools empower employees at all levels to identify opportunities for improvement, implement changes, and monitor results over time.

Automation Software
Automation software like Zapier, Microsoft Power Automate, or UiPath can automate repetitive tasks and streamline manual

processes. By automating routine tasks, teams can save time, reduce errors, and focus on higher-value activities.

Risk Management Tools

Risk management tools such as Risk Register or Risk Matrix help organizations identify, assess, and mitigate risks associated with change initiatives. These tools enable teams to proactively manage potential roadblocks and minimize their impact on project success.

Each tool has a purpose and may or may not be effective for different corporate cultures. You may need to conduct a needs assessment of your organization and pilot a few before launching to the whole system. It can feel very overwhelming to employees when too many tools are in use all at once. But by leveraging the right tools effectively, organizations can streamline processes, overcome roadblocks, and drive successful change initiatives more efficiently.

Have you ever encountered situations where silos within an organization hindered progress or collaboration? How did these silos manifest, and what impact did they have on achieving goals or completing projects effectively?

What are the most common barriers or roadblocks you face in your work environment when it comes to innovation and change? Are there existing processes or strategies in place to address and break down these barriers?

Celebrate Success

Professional soccer player Mia Hamm said, "Celebrate what you've accomplished, but raise the bar a little higher each time you succeed." Now retired, Hamm's contributions to women's soccer have left a lasting legacy and inspired generations of players around the world. She recognized the significance of celebrating success as it is essential for boosting morale, fostering a sense of accomplishment, and maintaining motivation among team members. Research has also reinforced the power of positive reinforcement and recognition in leadership, serving as potent motivators that boost morale, enhance motivation, and cultivate a sense of accomplishment among employees. Pioneering work by Amabile and Kramer, renowned researchers in the field of organizational psychology, shed light on how incremental progress in meaningful work profoundly influences employee motivation, creativity, and overall well-being. Their emphasis on acknowledging and celebrating small victories underscores their profound impact on employee morale and performance, reshaping our understanding of workplace dynamics and offering insights for leadership, organizational culture, and strategies for boosting employee engagement.

From the research, we now know that celebrating progress and success is not merely a gesture of acknowledgment but a fundamental aspect of fostering a culture of appreciation, recognition, and encouragement. While personal development initiatives and feedback mechanisms lay the groundwork for individual growth and improvement, celebrating progress and success serves as a catalyst for motivation, morale, and continued momentum towards achieving personal and organizational goals.

Conversely, there are those who do not leave space for celebrations at work and may label celebrations and recognition as "kum-ba-yah" or "childish". This can have horribly detrimental effects on workplace culture and employee morale. Such dismissive language undermines the importance of acknowledging achievements and milestones, which are essential for fostering a positive work environment. When celebrations are belittled in this way, employees may feel undervalued and unappreciated, leading to decreased motivation and engagement. Additionally, it perpetuates the misconception that emotions have no place in the workplace, stifling authentic expression and interpersonal connections. In reality, celebrating successes contributes to team cohesion, boosts morale, and reinforces desired behaviors, ultimately driving organizational success. What leads some individuals to overlook the importance of celebrating others' progress and performance, despite their own enjoyment of receiving praise and recognition for a job well done? It may be due to:

Fear of complacency
They may worry that celebrating wins could lead to a sense of complacency among employees, where they become content with their current achievements and stop striving for further improvement.

Concern about high expectations
They may fear that celebrating one win sets a precedent for expecting similar levels of success in the future, creating pressure to continually outperform previous accomplishments.

Belief in maintaining a focus on improvement
Some people may prioritize a continuous improvement mindset, believing that celebrating wins may divert attention away from identifying areas for growth and development.

Cultural or organizational norms
Certain organizational cultures may not prioritize or encourage celebration of wins, leading employees and their bosses to follow suit to align with established norms or expectations.

Personal insecurities
In certain instances, people might feel insecure about their own contributions to success, leading them to hesitate in celebrating wins for fear of diminishing their role or importance within the

organization. Additionally, they may worry about being perceived as lacking professionalism or emotionally soft if they openly celebrate victories.

Identifying these reasons can facilitate more productive discussions about the topic. After all, humans are hard wired to seek rewards due to the intricate workings of their brains, as evidenced by neuroscience and psychology. The brain's reward system, largely regulated by the release of dopamine, is pivotal in reinforcing behaviors vital for survival. When individuals experience something pleasurable or rewarding, such as accomplishing a task or receiving recognition, dopamine levels in the brain increase, creating feelings of satisfaction and pleasure. This reinforces the associated behavior, making it more likely to be repeated in the future.

Additionally, rewards activate the brain's limbic system, which is responsible for emotions and motivation, further fueling the desire to seek out rewarding experiences. From a psychological perspective, rewards serve as positive reinforcements that encourage desired behaviors and motivate individuals to pursue goals. They provide tangible evidence of progress and achievement, boosting confidence and self-esteem. Ultimately, understanding the neurological and psychological underpinnings of rewards can help leaders and organizations harness their power to drive motivation, productivity, and overall well-being.

Does this insinuate that everyone gets a participation ribbon? Not at all. There exists a balance between "everyone gets a trophy" with a militaristic approach. It requires finesse and practice, where discipline and acknowledgment harmonize. While a strict framework sets standards and fosters accountability, it's vital to recognize and reward efforts to maintain motivation and morale and recognition should be genuine, meaningful, and equitable. Effective leadership entails navigating this balance, encouraging growth through challenge while fostering a culture of appreciation and support, where individuals feel both driven to excel and valued for their contributions.

Recognizing progress, even with a simple "thank you," regardless of how small, reinforces the significance of individual efforts and contributions. By recognizing even the smallest achievements, organizations demonstrate their commitment to fostering a culture of appreciation and recognition. By publicly acknowledging achievements, organizations reinforce positive behaviors and attitudes, inspiring individuals to continue striving for excellence and pushing the boundaries of what is possible. This reinforcement of positive behaviors creates a virtuous cycle of motivation and achievement, driving sustained performance and success over time.

In addition to celebrating individual achievements, organizations should also cultivate a culture of collective celebration, where team successes are celebrated and shared across the organization. By highlighting the achievements of teams and departments, organizations can foster a sense of camaraderie, collaboration, and shared purpose, strengthening the fabric of the organization and building a sense of unity and cohesion among its members.

In your current work environment, how does your company recognize and celebrate successes or exceptional work? Are there existing practices or initiatives in place to acknowledge and reward employees for their contributions to innovation and positive change?

Do you feel that these practices effectively motivate and inspire employees to innovate and drive positive change? If not, what improvements or additional measures could be implemented to enhance the recognition and celebration of success within your company?

Learn from Failure & Reward Risk-Taking

Failure is an inevitable part of the innovation process, so in cultivating a thriving innovative culture, it's essential to embrace failure as a part of the learning process. But how do we do that when we have been conditioned to believe that failure is negative? When we fail, we often, if not always, feel shame and embarrassment. We are conditioned to perceive failure as a negative outcome rather than an opportunity for growth due to societal norms, cultural expectations, and personal experiences. From a young age, we are taught to equate success with achievement and perfection, while failure is stigmatized as a sign of inadequacy or incompetence. This mindset is often reinforced by educational systems that prioritize grades and test scores over the process of learning and experimentation.

Furthermore, societal pressures to conform to certain standards of success, particularly via social media, can foster a fear of failure, leading people to avoid taking risks or stepping outside of their comfort zones. This fear is exacerbated by a culture that values perfectionism and places a high emphasis on competition and comparison. Personal experiences of failure, especially when met with criticism or punishment, also contribute to a negative perception of failure. These experiences lead to an internalized belief that failure is inherently bad and should be avoided or hidden.

And not every change initiative will succeed. In fact, research suggests that nearly 70% of change initiatives fail! So, who's managing the 30%? According to a report by the Project Management Institute, the 30% are from resilient organizations that are better equipped to navigate challenges because they embody cultures of celebration and risk taking and see failure as a means to succeed. 73% of these resilient companies meet their goals more frequently and 80% successfully complete strategic initiatives over two years.

However, this doesn't imply celebrating when someone makes a significant mistake or blows the budget on a major project. Instead, it involves acknowledging what went well in the process and extracting valuable lessons to carry forward. This aids in building psychological safety, a key factor in promoting innovation and learning in organizations. As we know, teams with a high level of psychological safety are more likely to experiment, innovate, and grow. We can safely assume that the 30% of successful change initiatives identified in the research have cultures characterized by a high level of psychological safety.

And although we may claim to grasp these concepts, our brains might still function in counterproductive ways. When failure occurs, our brains engage in diverse psychological and neurological processes. Initially, there may be activation in regions associated with negative emotions such as the amygdala and insula, leading to these feelings of disappointment, frustration, and embarrassment. This activation triggers the release of stress hormones like cortisol, which can further intensify negative emotions and physiological arousal. Simultaneously, failure can also engage regions involved in self-reflection and cognitive processing, such as the prefrontal cortex. This part of the brain evaluates the situation, analyzes what went wrong, and considers potential alternative strategies or solutions.

This process of cognitive reappraisal and problem-solving is crucial for learning from failure and adapting future behavior. Over time, repeated experiences of failure and subsequent learning can lead to neuroplasticity, the brain's ability to reorganize and form new neural connections. Each time we experience failure and bounce back, our brain forms fresh patterns of resilience. As Winston Churchill once said, "Success is stumbling from failure to failure with no loss of enthusiasm". This belief will undoubtedly result in improved decision-making skills and more proactive and positive responses to future challenges.

Yet, we've all encountered individuals, whether at work or our personal lives, who find it difficult to overcome their failures and life challenges. Whether they openly admit it, they may dwell on past mistakes, avoid taking any risks, be reluctant to try new things, express fear or anxiety about failure, or display a lack of resilience in the face of setbacks. We know these people, so what factors are hindering neuroplasticity from reshaping their thought patterns? Several factors may be at play, including:

Chronic stress: Prolonged exposure to stress hormones like cortisol can impair neuroplasticity and lead to structural changes in the brain, particularly in areas involved in learning and memory.

Lack of stimulation: A sedentary lifestyle or lack of mental stimulation can deprive the brain of opportunities for growth and adaptation. Without new experiences and challenges to stimulate neural activity, neuroplasticity may be limited.

Poor sleep: Inadequate sleep can disrupt brain function and impair neuroplasticity. During sleep, the brain consolidates memories and processes information, essential for learning and synaptic plasticity.

Unhealthy lifestyle habits: Factors such as poor nutrition, substance abuse, and lack of physical activity can negatively impact brain health and inhibit neuroplasticity.

Aging: As we age, the brain's capacity for neuroplasticity naturally declines. However, engaging in mentally stimulating activities and leading a healthy lifestyle can help mitigate age-related declines in neuroplasticity.

Neurological conditions: Certain neurological conditions, such as stroke, traumatic brain injury, or neurodegenerative diseases, can disrupt neural networks and impair neuroplasticity. However, rehabilitation strategies and targeted interventions may help promote recovery and reorganization of brain function in some cases.

Only you can determine if you encounter obstacles in altering your brain's response to failure. Evaluate your surroundings and lifestyle: Are you maintaining a balanced, healthy routine, participating in mental and physical exercises, and coping with stress efficiently? Consider if colleagues or team members are grappling with similar challenges and how this awareness can aid you as a leader in navigating change effectively. These experiences present opportunities for growth and are vital for fostering neuroplasticity and sustaining optimal brain function throughout your life as you strive to assist others.

Think about your organization's attitude toward risk-taking and learning from failure. Are employees encouraged to take risks and experiment, or is there a prevailing aversion to failure?

How does your organization typically respond to failures or setbacks, and are there mechanisms in place to facilitate learning from these experiences?

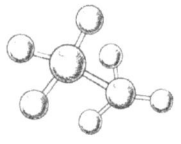

Part 3 Reflection

How can you apply the concept of learning from failure and adapting quickly within your own team or department to drive success?

What specific steps or strategies could you implement to foster a culture of experimentation and resilience?

Reflecting on your organization's current practices, what changes or improvements could you suggest to leadership to better promote a culture of learning from failure and agile adaptation?

How might these changes positively impact the organization's ability to innovate and achieve its goals?

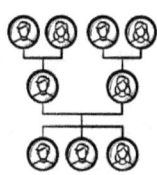

PART 4: COMMUNICATION MASTERY

Be Transparent and Authentic

Transparency and authenticity serve as cornerstones for building trust, fostering engagement, and nurturing a positive organizational culture. Deloitte researchers identified transparency, characterized by clear and straightforward communication of information, motives, and decisions relevant to employees, as a pivotal factor in building trust.

Transparency entails being forthcoming and honest in sharing information, whether it pertains to organizational goals, performance metrics, or upcoming changes. Leaders should strive to provide employees with a clear understanding of the organization's vision, strategy, and direction, helping them feel informed and engaged in the decision-making process. By openly communicating both successes and challenges, leaders demonstrate their commitment to honesty and integrity, laying the groundwork for a culture of trust and accountability.

Authenticity is also paramount in effective leadership. Authentic leaders are genuine, sincere, and true to themselves, fostering genuine connections and rapport with their teams. It involves being vulnerable and human, acknowledging both strengths and weaknesses, and leading with empathy and humility. When leaders show vulnerability and authenticity, they create an environment where employees feel comfortable sharing their thoughts, concerns, and ideas openly, fostering a culture of psychological safety and belonging.

Authentic leaders lead by example, embodying the values and principles they advocate for, thus inspiring others to follow suit. Through their actions and behaviors, these leaders create an environment where individuals feel empowered to express their true selves, fostering creativity and unleashing their full potential. Despite its benefits, many leaders struggle with authenticity due to the fear of appearing weak or vulnerable. However, research, such as that conducted by Brené Brown, reveals that vulnerability is not a sign of weakness but rather a strength. By embracing authenticity, leaders can cultivate trust, foster meaningful connections, and drive positive organizational change.

Conversely, when individuals believe they are authentic and transparent but are not, it often results in misalignment between their intentions and their actions. This discrepancy can lead to distrust and skepticism from others, as they may sense incongruence in the individual's behavior. It can also hinder effective communication and collaboration, as others may feel uncertain about the sincerity of the person's words and actions. Ultimately, failing to embody true authenticity and transparency can actually erode relationships and undermine leadership effectiveness.

Working with or for people who perceive themselves as authentic and transparent, but are not, can pose challenges. Recognizing key indicators will help navigate these difficult situations easier. Here are some tell-tale signs you may be working with an inauthentic individual:

Inconsistency between words and actions
If someone frequently espouses values like honesty and openness but demonstrates behavior that contradicts these principles, it may suggest a lack of authenticity and transparency.

How information is shared
Authentic and transparent leaders typically communicate openly, providing context and rationale behind decisions, whereas those who are not may withhold information or offer vague explanations.

How feedback is received
Authentic leaders welcome constructive criticism and are willing to acknowledge their shortcomings, whereas those lacking in

authenticity may become defensive or dismissive when confronted with feedback.

The degree to which people are aware of their behavior or care about it varies greatly depending on the person and the situation. Some people may be fully aware of their inauthenticity or tendency to withhold information but choose to continue their behavior for personal gain or protection. Others may be unaware of how their actions are perceived by others and may genuinely believe they are acting authentically. Additionally, some may care deeply about their reputation and relationships and may be open to feedback and self-reflection to improve their behavior. In the end, supporting others' growth doesn't require knowing every detail about them. It's about approaching each situation with empathy and understanding, acknowledging the diverse motivations and perspectives among individuals.

How do you currently prioritize transparency and authenticity in your communications with your team?

How do you believe trust influences performance in the workplace? Can you think of an experience where a lack of trust hindered productivity or collaboration, or conversely, where a strong foundation of trust led to exceptional performance and outcomes?

Can you recall a time when a leader's transparency and authenticity (or lack thereof) directly impacted others around them?

Practice Active Listening

Active listening emerges as a vital skill for leaders seeking to foster meaningful connections, nurture relationships, and drive engagement within their teams. Active listening goes beyond the mere act of hearing words; it involves fully immersing oneself in the speaker's message, both verbally and nonverbally. Neuroscientist Dr. David Rock's comprehensive studies on the human brain illuminate how it reacts to social interactions. His research demonstrates that active listening can profoundly influence the brain's neural pathways, resulting in enhanced communication, strengthened relationships, and heightened productivity. Rock also found that when individuals feel heard and understood, their brains release dopamine, similar to being praised and rewarded. Consequently, this can foster a favorable connection with the listener, forging a more solid bond and a stronger professional relationship.

However, active listening can be challenging. In today's fast-paced and technology-driven world with constant distractions and disruptions, it can be difficult for us to give our full attention to others. Moreover, inherent biases and preconceptions can cloud even the best listener's ability to truly hear and understand the speaker's message. Additionally, the pressure to respond quickly or provide solutions may lead to a lack of patience and attentiveness in listening. Here are steps to practice active listening:

Give Your Full Attention
Especially when it's an important conversation, eliminate distractions such as phones or side conversations. Maintain comfortable eye contact and focus on the speaker's words, tone, and body language. In remote settings where interactions occur over video calls, resist the urge to check emails or read chat messages. By prioritizing active engagement during remote discussions, leaders uphold the principles of respect and

attentiveness, ensuring that team members feel valued and supported regardless of the communication medium.

Paraphrase and Reflect

After the speaker has finished expressing themselves, paraphrase what they said to ensure you understood correctly. By reflecting back the speaker's message in their own words, leaders validate the speaker's perspective and foster mutual understanding. While books often portray paraphrasing and reflection as simple and scripted techniques, they involve more than just repeating words verbatim. True validation come from deeply understanding the speaker's emotions, concerns, and intentions, and reflecting these back in a genuine and authentic manner. It requires a sensitivity to nonverbal cues, and a genuine desire to connect with the speaker on a meaningful level. Therefore, while the concept may seem straightforward in theory, executing it effectively requires practice, intuition, and a commitment to understanding others.

Find the Right Balance

Although usually well-intended, some people respond to stories by immediately shifting the focus to themselves, and this may make the speaker feel invalidated or unheard, as their experience is being overshadowed by the listener's desire to share their own. This can lead to feelings of frustration or resentment, especially if the speaker was seeking support or validation. Additionally, it can disrupt the flow of conversation and prevent deeper understanding or connection between the speaker and listener. While it's natural for people to relate to stories based on their own experiences, it's important to balance this with active listening and genuine empathy for the speaker's perspective.

Ask Questions

Questions in active listening serve not only to demonstrate genuine interest and engagement but also to uncover any underlying issues or concerns the speaker may have. By asking thoughtful questions, you can uncover hidden motivations, emotions, or challenges that may not be immediately apparent. This allows you to provide more meaningful support or guidance.

Avoid Interrupting

Allow the speaker to express themselves fully without interruption. Avoid jumping in with your own thoughts or opinions before they have finished speaking. I know it's challenging but understanding why you do it may help you stop doing it. Consider if any of the following resonate with you as reasons for interrupting:

Impatience

You don't want to lose an important point and jump to express your thoughts or opinions without waiting for the speaker to finish. Being impatient can often lead to impulsivity and a tendency to interrupt others during conversations or meetings. This behavior can create a sense of frustration for both the impatient individual and those they interrupt though, as it disrupts the flow of communication and undermines the value of active listening and can contribute to heightened stress levels and a sense of disconnection.

Eagerness

You are excited or enthusiastic about the topic and want to contribute immediately. It's important to remember that even if you're knowledgeable about the topic at hand and eager to contribute, you don't have to share everything all at once. By waiting and allowing others to share their experiences and opinions, you can create a more inclusive and respectful dialogue. If the timing is right and your input can enhance the conversation, you'll have a more meaningful impact by patiently waiting for your turn to speak.

Lack of Awareness

This can stem from various factors, including not being fully attuned to the nuances of others' communication styles. For example, you might misinterpret a brief pause in someone's speech as a sign that they have finished speaking, prompting you to jump in prematurely. In reality, they may have simply been taking a moment to gather their thoughts before continuing their train of thought. This lack of awareness can lead to interruptions and miscommunications, as well as a failure to fully appreciate the perspectives and contributions of others in the conversation. Therefore, developing greater awareness of both verbal and nonverbal cues in communication is essential for fostering effective and respectful dialogue.

Control

In the context of active listening, the desire for control can undermine the effectiveness of communication. When individuals seek to assert dominance or steer the conversation in their preferred direction, they may monopolize the discussion, interrupt others, or dismiss alternative viewpoints. This behavior not only hampers genuine understanding but also erodes trust and collaboration within the group. To foster active listening, it's important to cultivate a mindset of openness and humility, valuing the contributions of others and allowing space for diverse perspectives to be heard and respected. By relinquishing the need for control and embracing a more inclusive approach to communication, individuals can create environments where genuine dialogue and mutual understanding thrive.

Cultural differences

Cultural differences can clearly influence this behavior, as norms surrounding interruption can vary widely between different cultures. For instance, in some cultures, interrupting during a conversation is seen as a sign of engagement and active participation, while in others, it may be perceived as disrespectful or rude. Recognizing and respecting these cultural nuances is essential for effective communication across diverse teams and environments.

Active listening is a pivotal skill for leaders, one that extends beyond merely hearing words to deeply understanding the thoughts, feelings, and concerns of those they lead. By actively listening, leaders demonstrate respect and empathy, building trust and rapport within the organization. Additionally, active listening allows leaders to gather valuable insights and perspectives, enabling them to make more informed decisions and navigate challenges effectively. Ultimately, leaders who master the art of active listening inspire loyalty, engagement, and high performance among their teams, driving success for the organization as a whole.

Are you aware of your own listening strengths and weaknesses?

Reflecting on your recent conversations, how often do you find yourself actively listening versus simply waiting for your turn to speak?

What specific steps can you take to be a stronger listener as you develop your own leadership style?

Embrace Empathy

Active listening requires leaders to cultivate empathy and understanding towards the speaker's perspective and emotions. Empathy is the ability to understand and share the feelings of others. It involves putting oneself in someone else's shoes, seeing things from their perspective, and experiencing their emotions. In recent years, empathy has become a buzzword in various fields, including leadership, psychology, and business, due to its profound impact on relationships, communication, and teamwork. As organizations recognize the importance of creating inclusive and supportive environments, it has emerged as a key skill for leaders and team members alike.

Empathetic leaders are better able to connect with their employees, build trust, and foster a sense of belonging within the organization. Empathy enables individuals to navigate conflicts more effectively, resolve differences, and collaborate productively. In today's fast-paced and interconnected world, where understanding and connecting with others is essential for success, it has rightfully taken center stage as a critical skill for personal and professional growth. By acknowledging and validating the speaker's emotions, leaders create a safe and supportive space for open dialogue and honest communication. This, in turn, strengthens relationships, builds rapport, and enhances team cohesion.

But let's be honest for a minute. Empathy can sometimes be challenging for us to cultivate, especially in certain situations or with certain people. One factor that can impede empathy is a lack of understanding or awareness of the other person's perspective or experiences. If you find it difficult to relate to or comprehend the emotions or circumstances of another person, it becomes challenging for you to empathize. Understanding how your personal biases, prejudices, or stereotypes can impede your empathy is crucial in maintaining professional relationships. These factors can erect barriers between you and others, making it challenging to establish genuine emotional connections. Disparities in background, upbringing, or cultural norms further contribute to these disconnects. Emotional barriers such as fear, discomfort, or emotional overload can also interfere. As we acknowledge the influence of the amygdala, it's important to understand that when individuals are overwhelmed by their own emotions or grappling with personal challenges, self-preservation often takes precedence. In such moments, the capacity to empathize with others may be compromised, as attention is directed inward rather than outward.

It has always been helpful for me to consider Maslow's Hierarchy of Needs, a psychological model proposed by Abraham Maslow in 1943. Often depicted as a pyramid, basic physiological needs are at the base and higher-level needs such as self-actualization are at the top. The theory suggests that individuals are motivated to fulfill these needs in a hierarchical order, with lower-level needs taking precedence before higher-level needs can be addressed. Maslow's model has been influential in psychology and related fields, shaping our understanding of human motivation and behavior and reminds us that addressing our own emotional well-being is essential before we can effectively support others. By prioritizing self-care and recognizing when we need to take a step back to manage our own emotions, we can then better empathize with and support our team members in navigating their own challenges and growth.

In addition to self-improvement, learning about fundamental psychological theories can help leaders at any level because they provide valuable insights into human behavior and motivation, which are essential for effective leadership. In addition to Maslow's Hierarchy of Needs, other theories such as Herzberg's Two-Factor Theory, which distinguishes between hygiene factors (such as salary and working conditions) and motivators (such as recognition and achievement), and Vroom's Expectancy Theory, which suggests that motivation depends on the belief that effort will lead to performance and performance will lead to desired outcomes, are also relevant when digging into empathy in the workplace. By understanding and applying these theories, leaders can create environments that promote employee well-being, motivation, and productivity, ultimately leading to the success of both individuals and organizational transformation.

But here's the biggest takeaway. To be a great leader, you don't need to know every detail of people's lives to understand that they've all experienced challenges and growth. Part of the MindShift Effect involves confronting and questioning concepts and barriers, encouraging you to approach situations and interact with people in new and unconventional ways. To achieve this, you must dig deep into self-awareness, which can be uncomfortable at times, but that's where true empathy comes from.

What do you think might be the biggest obstacle for you in cultivating empathy in certain situations?

What specific steps do you believe you can take to overcome any barriers hindering your ability to empathize effectively in challenging situations?

Adapt Your Communication Style

Effective communication serves as the linchpin that binds teams together, drives collaboration, and propels organizations toward success. And although we touched on this a bit earlier, it is relevant in this section because communicating effectively is not a one-size-fits-all endeavor. Rather, it demands a nuanced understanding of the diverse needs, preferences, and contexts that shape interpersonal interactions. Research has shown that adaptability in communication style is crucial for leaders to connect with their teams, foster engagement, and inspire action. It involves tailoring communication approaches to meet the needs and preferences of different individuals and situations. Here are some key points to consider:

Understand Your Audience Needs
Leading is not about doing all the talking, nor is it about always having all the answers. Leaders should actively listen to their team members, observe their communication styles, and solicit feedback to understand their preferences. It's important to recognize that everyone has their own preconceived notions about anything and everything, and as a leader, you can't read their minds. Therefore, applying active listening skills is crucial to truly understand what they have to offer and what they need.

Tailor Your Communication Approach
Leaders can adapt their communication style, tone, and delivery according to the preferences of their audience to ensure better resonance and understanding. And tone – the most powerful factor in communication. Tone is paramount. Two individuals can convey the exact same message and elicit vastly different responses solely based on tone. Consider how you want a message to be received and whether your tone aligns with that intention.

Be Flexible in Verbal and Nonverbal Communication
Effective communication goes beyond words; leaders should also be attuned to nonverbal cues such as body language, facial expressions, and gestures. These cues often provide valuable insights into the thoughts and emotions of others, allowing leaders to better understand their team members' perspectives and concerns.

Build Rapport and Trust
By demonstrating sensitivity and empathy in their communication, leaders can foster deeper connections and understanding with their audience. This includes active listening and being authentic and transparent in your responses and day-to-day communication.

Just like leadership, communication is not a one-size-fits-all endeavor. I once had a boss with a very straightforward communication style, which some might even describe as abrasive. He made it clear to the entire company that he wasn't willing to change his approach for anyone, stating, "This is just the way it is. If you don't like it, tough. I change for no one". While a few employees found his honesty to be refreshing, the majority found his demeanor polarizing and off-putting. He became seen as an unapproachable leader, unwilling to adapt his communication style or behaviors to meet the needs of others, and ultimately alienated many employees, inhibiting trust and collaboration, breaking down the protective walls of psychological safety that were once there.

The most effective and influential leaders do the exact opposite. They recognize the importance of adaptability and empathy in communication. Rather than insisting on their own way, they listen to others, are willing to adjust their approach, and foster an environment of trust and collaboration. By demonstrating flexibility and understanding, these leaders create stronger connections with their employees, leading to higher levels of engagement and productivity.

How do you perceive the impact of tone of voice on the effectiveness of a message? Can you recall a specific instance where the tone of voice played a significant role in either reinforcing or diminishing the message's impact?

How do you currently adapt your communication style to meet the diverse needs and preferences of your team?

Provide Constructive Feedback

In the intricacy of leadership, the art of providing constructive feedback emerges as a cornerstone for nurturing talent, fostering growth, and propelling teams through successful change. Feedback serves as a guiding light, illuminates areas of strength and areas for improvement, and paves the way for continuous learning and development.

However, providing constructive feedback can be challenging, as it requires finesse and clarity. After all, just hearing, "Can you come talk for second? I have some feedback for you" can elicit a negative neurological response. Similar to the word "failure", the term "feedback" often evokes negative neurological responses in the brain, and some people immediately anticipate criticism or correction. Regions of the brain associated with stress and threat detection, such as the amygdala and the anterior cingulate cortex, become activated, triggering the release of the stress hormone cortisol, leading to feelings of anxiety, defensiveness, or even avoidance behavior. Overall, the neurological response to feedback highlights the complex interplay between cognitive, emotional, and physiological processes in the human brain and that's why it can be so difficult to offer.

For years, people were encouraged to use the sandwich method for feedback as a means to make the process easier and less painful. We now know this is not as effective as we once believed. This approach involves sandwiching constructive criticism between layers of praise or positive feedback. While this method was well-intended, it has several drawbacks that can undermine its effectiveness. The sandwich method can:

Come across as insincere or manipulative
When feedback is sandwiched between positive remarks, recipients may perceive it as disingenuous or sugar-coating, leading to skepticism about the genuine nature of the praise.

Dilute the impact of constructive feedback
By burying criticism between layers of positivity, the intended message may be softened or obscured, making it less likely to resonate with the recipient or spur meaningful change.

Create confusion or mixed signals
Recipients may focus more on the positive aspects of the feedback and overlook the areas requiring improvement, or vice versa. This lack of clarity can hinder the recipient's ability to understand and act upon the feedback effectively.

Reinforce a culture of avoidance or reluctance
Instead of fostering open and honest communication, it may encourage individuals to shy away from giving or receiving candid feedback, perpetuating underlying problems rather than resolving them.

So, while offering a balance of positive and constructive feedback is important, the sandwich method may not be the most effective or genuine approach. To provide constructive feedback effectively, leaders should adopt a multi-faceted approach that encompasses both formal and informal feedback mechanisms. Regular feedback sessions, such as performance reviews or one-on-one meetings, provide structured opportunities for discussing strengths, areas for improvement, and developmental goals. During these sessions, leaders should strive to be specific and concrete in their feedback, citing examples and providing actionable suggestions for improvement. There should never be surprises at year-end reviews; employees should have a clear understanding of their performance throughout the year, with ongoing feedback and guidance from their leaders. This approach fosters transparency, trust, and accountability, leading to more meaningful and productive discussions during annual reviews.

In addition to formal feedback sessions, leaders should also embrace informal feedback opportunities that arise during day-to-day interactions. Whether it's a quick check-in after a team meeting or a brief conversation in the hallway or virtually, these informal moments offer valuable opportunities to provide real-time feedback and recognition. By seizing these opportunities, you will demonstrate your commitment to employee development and reinforce positive behaviors as they occur.

Furthermore, the delivery of constructive feedback should be accompanied by support, encouragement, and empathy. Acknowledge the effort and progress made while providing guidance for improvement. By adopting a supportive stance, leaders can create a safe and trusting environment where individuals feel empowered to take risks and pursue growth opportunities. Feedback doesn't have to feel formal or over-scripted either. Here are some tips if you struggle to get feedback off the ground:

- I've been thinking about [specific situation or project], and I wanted to share some thoughts...

- I've noticed [specific behavior or action], and I think it's worth discussing...

- Can we talk about [specific topic or issue]? I have some ideas I'd like to bounce off you...

- I appreciate how [specific action or effort], and I have a suggestion for how we could build on that...

- I've been reflecting on [specific outcome or result], and I think there's an opportunity for improvement...

- I've noticed a pattern of [specific behavior or trend], and I believe addressing it could benefit our team...

- I wanted to touch base about [specific goal or objective], and discuss any adjustments or strategies moving forward...

And the most powerful one:

- I'd like to hear your thoughts on [specific goal or behavior]. How do you think it went?

While it may initially be time-consuming and uncomfortable for some managers, the absence of ongoing, consistent feedback can have a profoundly negative impact. Without regular feedback, employees may struggle to understand their performance expectations, leading to uncertainty and decreased job satisfaction. This lack of clarity can hinder professional growth and development, as employees may not receive the guidance needed to improve their skills or address areas of weakness. The absence of feedback can also erode trust between employees and managers, as it may signal a lack of interest or investment in their success. Over time, this can contribute to disengagement, increased turnover rates, and decreased morale within the workforce.

Providing constructive feedback is vital to being an effective leader. By offering timely, specific, and actionable feedback, leaders can empower their team members to reach their full potential, drive performance, and achieve collective success. People generally crave feedback and if you present it as an opportunity for improvement rather than criticism or discouragement, you are halfway there.

How do you approach giving constructive feedback to others? Do you tend to address issues promptly and constructively, or do you find yourself avoiding difficult conversations and hoping the issue will resolve itself over time?

When you do offer feedback to someone, how do you ensure your message is delivered constructively and positively, fostering growth rather than discouragement?

Be Clear and Concise

Research has consistently shown that clear and concise communication enhances understanding, alignment, and engagement among employees. Therefore, leaders must prioritize clarity and simplicity in their communications to ensure that messages are easily understood and actionable. In today's fast-paced business environment though, employees are inundated with information from so many sources, making it essential for leaders to cut through the noise and deliver messages that are relevant and impactful. By distilling complex ideas into concise and easily digestible nuggets of information, leaders can capture the attention of their audience and ensure that their messages are heard and understood.

In the workplace, I've noticed that overcommunication is often as common as individuals working in isolation or failing to communicate altogether. This can result in people feeling overwhelmed and shutting down, or simply ignoring messages due to cognitive overload. As this is a frequent issue, let's explore several explanations for over-communicating:

Insecurity: Some individuals may lack confidence in their ability to convey their message effectively, so they compensate by providing excessive detail or explanation. They may worry that they haven't expressed themselves clearly enough and believe that adding more words will help clarify their message.

Fear of being misunderstood: There's often a fear of not being understood or of leaving out important information, so people may err on the side of over-explaining to ensure nothing is missed. They may believe that providing more information reduces the likelihood of misinterpretation.

Pressure to impress: In some cases, individuals may feel pressure to impress their audience, whether it's a boss, colleague, or client. They may mistakenly believe that demonstrating their knowledge or expertise through verbose communication will enhance their credibility or perceived competence.

Habit: Some people may simply have a habit of being verbose in their communication. Perhaps they've received positive feedback in the past for being thorough, or they've developed a writing style that leans towards verbosity.

Lack of editing or self-awareness: Without proper self-editing or awareness of their communication style, individuals may continue to "vomit words" onto the page without realizing it. They may not recognize when their message has become unnecessarily long or convoluted.

If any of these situations strike a chord with you or bring someone to mind in your workplace, you're not alone. Striking the right balance can be challenging, and effective communication is a skill that demands practice. Being clear and concise while avoiding overwhelming the audience with unnecessary detail is not easy. Moreover, each individual possesses a unique style. However, staying focused on the objective and purpose behind your message and seeking feedback from respected peers can be invaluable.

In an era dominated by texting and abbreviations, communication has also become increasingly casual. Consequently, many individuals, including experienced professionals, struggle with maintaining strong writing skills. I once worked with a senior leader whose forté wasn't conventional grammar. She often misspelled words, mishandled capitalization, and struggled with punctuation. Does that disqualify her from being effective in her role? Depending on her position, not necessarily. However, when she sent emails to vendors and stakeholders without proofreading, despite her manager's advice to do so, it became an issue. Why does it matter if she could perform the rest of her job well? Research indicates that we form impressions based on people's writing, particularly in a professional context. And according to Forbes, fewer grammatical errors correlate with more promotions. They found that professionals with 6-9 promotions made 45% fewer grammatical errors than those who'd been promoted 1-4 times!

The good news is there are several tools available to help improve clarity and conciseness in writing, if it's for more than just a Teams or Slack chat:

Grammarly
Grammarly is a writing assistant that helps identify grammatical errors, awkward phrasing, and wordiness. It provides suggestions for improving clarity and conciseness in your writing.

Hemingway Editor
Hemingway Editor highlights complex sentences, passive voice, and excessive adverbs, helping you simplify your writing for greater clarity.

WordRake
WordRake is a proofreading software that suggests edits to remove unnecessary words and improve clarity in your writing.

Plain Language Checker
At minimum, do a spell and grammar check and see what suggestions there are for simpler alternatives and improved clarity.

Trusted Colleagues
Turning to trusted colleagues who are strong writers and communicators to proofread your work before it goes out can greatly enhance its quality and effectiveness.

By utilizing these tools, you can streamline your writing, eliminate unnecessary words, and ensure that your message is communicated clearly and effectively. By prioritizing clarity and simplicity in your communications, you can ensure that your messages resonate with employees, drive alignment, and inspire action. Ultimately, clear and concise communication lays the foundation for a culture of professionalism, trust, and success within an organization.

How well do you understand your strengths and weaknesses in written communication? Can you identify specific areas where you excel and others where you might benefit from improvement?

When crafting your message to convey important information, how do you ensure clarity and conciseness without sacrificing the depth or relevance of the content?

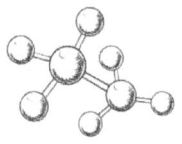

Part 4 Reflection

How can leaders ensure that transparency and authenticity are not just buzzwords but deeply ingrained principles in their organizational culture?

Reflecting on your recent interactions with colleagues or team members, how have you demonstrated authenticity in your leadership approach in a world where communication channels are constantly evolving, and individuals have diverse preferences for receiving information?

How can leaders adapt their communication styles to effectively engage with their team members?

What strategies or techniques can leaders employ to ensure their messages are clear, concise, and relevant, resonating with employees across various channels and platforms?

PART 5: UNLOCKING POTENTIAL

Unlock Potential

Unlocking potential refers to the process of discovering and maximizing one's capabilities, talents, and strengths to achieve personal or professional goals. It involves recognizing and cultivating innate abilities, as well as developing new skills and competencies. Unlocking potential often entails overcoming obstacles, expanding boundaries, and tapping into previously untapped resources or opportunities. This process involves self-discovery, learning, growth, and continuous improvement. Ultimately, it empowers individuals to realize their fullest possible selves and to make meaningful contributions to their own lives and the world around them.

In the context of work, it's important to explore methods for unlocking potential in both group and individual settings, mirroring the realities of professional environments. In group settings, individuals benefit from collective knowledge, diverse perspectives, and collaborative problem-solving, which can lead to innovative ideas and creative solutions. Group dynamics such as social support, peer encouragement, and shared accountability can motivate individuals to push their boundaries and explore new possibilities, fostering a sense of belonging and collective achievement. However, group settings can also present challenges, including conformity pressures, social hierarchies, and conflicts of interest, which may inhibit individual expression and limit the exploration of diverse perspectives.

On the other hand, individual settings offer autonomy, self-directed learning, and personalized attention, allowing individuals to focus on their unique strengths, interests, and goals. In individual settings, people have the freedom to explore their full potential without the influence of group dynamics or external expectations. However, individual settings may lack the richness of social interaction and collaborative learning found in group settings, potentially limiting exposure to diverse ideas and perspectives. Overall, both group and individual settings play vital roles in unlocking potential, and the most effective approaches often involve a balanced integration of both contexts, leveraging the strengths of each to optimize personal and collective growth. In this chapter, we will explore techniques for unlocking both individual and organizational potential, exploring the role of mindset shifts, goal setting, and personal development.

Unlocking *your* potential begins with fostering a growth mindset. By cultivating a growth mindset, you can overcome self-limiting beliefs, which requires a significant amount of work, insight, and reflection. It involves being open to opinions, embracing challenges as opportunities for growth, and persisting in the face of setbacks. Additionally, self-awareness plays a crucial role in this process, as you must understand your strengths, weaknesses, values, and goals to effectively chart your path toward personal and professional development. And just to say we are self-aware doesn't make it so. We are truly only self-aware when we engage in honest introspection, seeking to understand our thoughts, emotions, and behaviors without judgment or bias. This requires a willingness to confront uncomfortable truths about ourselves and to actively seek feedback from others. Through this process, we gain a deeper understanding of who we are, what drives us, and how we can continue to grow and evolve. True self-awareness empowers us to make informed decisions, build meaningful relationships, and unlock our full potential.

How can organizations effectively balance individual autonomy and collective collaboration to maximize overall effectiveness, particularly in the evolving landscape of hybrid work environments?

Embrace a Growth Mindset

Embracing a growth mindset emerges as a pivotal strategy for fostering personal and professional development within teams. It recognizes the inherent potential for growth and learning in every individual, emphasizing the power of effort and persistence in achieving success.

A growth mindset is the belief that:

- Intelligence, abilities, and talents can be developed through dedication, effort, and learning.

- Challenges are embraced as opportunities.

- Persistence is the best action in the face of setbacks.

- To improve, you must seek out feedback and learn from it.

- The success of others is as inspiring as our own successes.

- Failure is just a steppingstone toward mastery.

- Skills can be honed through practice and perseverance.

- Resilience, motivation, and achievement are personal and professional endeavors.

On the contrary, a fixed mindset is the belief that:

- Intelligence, abilities, and talents are fixed traits.

- Challenges should be avoided to maintain a sense of competence.

- In the face of obstacles, giving up is an acceptable option.

- Feedback is not necessary or wanted.

- Others' success is a threat.

- Failure is due to inherent limitations or circumstances out of their control.

These factors contribute to diminished resilience, motivation, and achievement in both personal and professional pursuits. Consider individuals you've encountered who adopt a victim mentality. Those who consistently portray themselves as victims of circumstance are not usually the ones you think of as inspiring and influential leaders.

It is important to note that having a growth mindset does not equate to toxic positivity. Instead, it's about acknowledging the reality of challenges while maintaining a belief in one's ability to overcome them. While a growth mindset encourages optimism and resilience, it also recognizes the importance of facing difficulties head-on and learning from them. It's not about dismissing negative emotions or pretending that everything is perfect. Rather, it's about reframing setbacks as opportunities for growth and finding constructive ways to address them. By embracing both the positive and negative aspects of life, individuals with a growth mindset can cultivate a balanced perspective that fosters personal and professional development in the long run.

And remember, authenticity is crucial for leaders to remember. Even when well-intended, coming across as a robotic or scripted optimist can be harmful, giving the impression that you are hiding something. When you display toxic positivity, people will see right through it. It's okay to say to your team, "This is rough. It's a challenging time. I feel it too," because you're acknowledging their human emotions while also stepping up with solutions and creating an environment of trust. Especially during periods of significant change within the company, where not all transitions have been positive, expressing unwavering, daily positivity may not resonate well with your team.

Like anything in life, it's all about finding that balance. You don't want to be like Eeyore, gloomy and pessimistic, especially when people are already struggling, and they are looking at you for guidance. But at the same time, you don't want to be bouncing around like Tigger, overly cheerful and insensitive to the challenges others are facing, even if your intentions are good. Striking that middle ground, where you acknowledge the difficulties while also offering support and solutions, is key.

How conscious are you of your own mindset tendencies, particularly between a growth and fixed mindset?

Can you recall instances where your mindset influenced your approach to challenges or opportunities?

Set Goals

Establishing a process for setting goals, tracking progress, and measuring success is vital for companies to grow and thrive. A meta-analysis conducted by renowned psychologists Locke and Latham found that setting clear and challenging goals enhances performance. Through various experiments and studies, they demonstrated that specific, difficult goals direct attention, increase effort, promote persistence, and stimulate the development of strategies to achieve them. Their work also emphasizes the importance of feedback, task complexity, and goal commitment in goal attainment, highlighting the role of self-regulation processes such as planning and monitoring progress in achieving goals.

The effectiveness of goal-setting strategies can vary greatly though depending on factors such as company size, organizational culture, specific needs, and age of the organization. There's no one-size-fits-all approach; rather, companies must identify the strategy that aligns best with their unique circumstances and objectives.

Regardless of these factors, without a framework in place, organizations may find themselves adrift, lacking direction and clarity on their objectives and approaches to change. This lack of structure can lead to inefficiencies, missed opportunities, and a disconnect between individual efforts and overarching company goals. Additionally, without a clear means of assessing progress and outcomes, companies risk stagnation, falling behind competitors, and failing to meet the evolving needs of their stakeholders.

OKRs

OKRs, or Objectives and Key Results, serve as a goal-setting framework used by organizations to define and track objectives and their corresponding outcomes. If you are new to the concept, I recommend *Measure What Matters* by John Doerr; it's like a roadmap for organizations, and shows how to set goals, measure progress effectively, and it's not just about numbers. It's about inspiring teams to strive for big, meaningful objectives and tracking their journey with measurable key results. This approach isn't just theory either; it's backed by real success stories from companies like Google and Intel.

Objectives are ambitious, qualitative goals that articulate what the organization aims to achieve, providing direction and purpose. Key Results are specific, measurable outcomes that indicate progress toward the objectives, defining the metrics and milestones that signify success. Together, they create a roadmap for the organization, guiding teams and individuals in their efforts to contribute to overarching goals.

One of the primary benefits of OKRs is their ability to promote alignment and focus throughout the organization. By setting clear objectives and measurable key results, OKRs ensure that everyone understands the organization's priorities and works toward common goals. This alignment helps to increase efficiency, minimize wasted effort, and maximize impact. Additionally, OKRs foster transparency and accountability, as progress toward objectives is tracked and shared openly, enabling teams to celebrate successes and address challenges collaboratively.

However, OKRs also come with some potential drawbacks. One challenge is ensuring that objectives are sufficiently ambitious but still achievable. Setting overly ambitious goals can lead to frustration and demotivation if they're perceived as unattainable. Conversely, setting goals that are too easy may not inspire the necessary effort and innovation and there can also be a tendency to focus solely on achieving the key results, sometimes at the expense of broader organizational objectives. This can lead to a narrow, short-term focus that overlooks the bigger picture. Overall, while OKRs offer numerous benefits in terms of alignment, focus, and accountability, they require careful planning and execution to realize their full potential.

KPIs

KPIs, or Key Performance Indicators, are specific metrics used by organizations to evaluate their performance and progress toward strategic objectives. Unlike OKRs, which focus on setting ambitious goals and defining measurable outcomes, KPIs are typically more focused on monitoring and assessing ongoing performance in various areas of the organization. KPIs can vary widely depending on the organization's goals and priorities but often include metrics related to financial performance, operational efficiency, customer satisfaction, and employee productivity.

One of the main benefits of KPIs is their ability to provide organizations with valuable insights into their performance and help identify areas for improvement. By tracking key metrics over time, organizations can measure their success against predefined benchmarks or targets, enabling them to make informed decisions and adjustments as needed. Additionally, KPIs can help align individual and team efforts with broader organizational objectives, ensuring that everyone is working toward common goals and priorities.

Like OKRs, KPIs also have some possible disadvantages. One challenge is selecting the right KPIs that accurately reflect the organization's goals and priorities. If KPIs are not carefully chosen or are too narrowly focused, they may fail to provide a comprehensive view of performance or overlook important aspects of the business. There can also be a tendency to become overly reliant on KPIs as the sole measure of success, which may lead to a narrow, short-term focus at the expense of long-term strategic objectives. Finally, measuring and tracking KPIs requires time and resources, and organizations may struggle to collect accurate data or integrate disparate systems effectively. Despite these challenges, KPIs remain a valuable tool for monitoring performance and driving organizational improvement when used thoughtfully and in conjunction with other performance management strategies.

SMART Goals

SMART goals are a framework for setting objectives that are Specific, Measurable, Achievable, Relevant, and Time-bound. Specific goals clearly define what is to be achieved, leaving no room for ambiguity or interpretation. Measurable goals are quantifiable, allowing progress to be tracked and evaluated objectively. Achievable objectives are practical and reachable, considering the available resources and limitations. Relevant goals align with the organization's mission, values, and strategic priorities, contributing directly to its overall success. Time-bound goals have a defined timeline or deadline, providing a sense of accountability and urgency.

One of the primary benefits of SMART goals is their clarity and specificity, which helps ensure that everyone involved understands exactly what is expected and how success will be measured. This clarity fosters alignment and focus, enabling individuals and teams to direct their efforts toward achieving the desired outcomes. The measurable aspect of SMART goals allows progress to be tracked and evaluated objectively, providing valuable feedback and insights into performance. SMART goals also promote accountability by establishing clear deadlines and milestones, encouraging individuals to take ownership of their work and results.

However, one challenge is that the emphasis on measurability and achievability may lead to a focus on short-term, easily attainable objectives at the expense of more ambitious, long-term goals. Additionally, the rigid structure of SMART goals may not always be suitable for complex or innovative projects that require flexibility and adaptability. Finally, the SMART framework may be overly prescriptive in some cases, limiting creativity and innovation by imposing strict criteria for goal setting. Despite these limitations, SMART goals remain a widely used and effective tool for setting clear objectives and driving performance improvement in organizations.

Certainly, the process of goal setting doesn't have to dominate every aspect of your work, nor does it require a rigid, militaristic approach. However, having a structured system in place is essential for providing clarity and direction, especially during times of significant transformation. As you might relate, I vividly recall a former boss – the same one who said he wouldn't change for anyone – completely dismiss OKRs and disregard them thereafter. I think his exact words were, "If I could throw them out yesterday, I would". While my initial reaction was to immediately argue the potential risks of his opinion, I later contemplated the reasons behind his strong stance. Here's what I uncovered. Several factors can lead individuals to avoid setting goals:

Fear of Failure
Some people may avoid setting goals because they fear falling short or not achieving them, even executives who have years of experience. The fear of failure can be paralyzing, leading individuals to avoid goal setting altogether rather than risk disappointment or embarrassment.

Lack of Clarity
Setting goals requires a clear understanding of one's priorities, values, and aspirations. Individuals who lack clarity about what they want to achieve or how to get there may feel overwhelmed or uncertain, making goal setting seem daunting or unattainable.

Comfort with the Status Quo
Change can be uncomfortable, and setting goals often entails stepping out of one's comfort zone and embracing new challenges. Individuals who are content with their current circumstances may see little value in setting goals, preferring to maintain the status quo rather than pursue growth or development.

Perceived Lack of Control
Some people may believe that external factors or circumstances beyond their control heavily influence their outcomes. In such cases, individuals may question the efficacy of setting goals, feeling that their efforts won't make a significant difference in the face of external forces.

Negative Past Experiences
Previous setbacks or failures in goal pursuit can dampen enthusiasm and confidence, leading individuals to adopt a more cautious approach or avoid setting goals altogether to shield themselves from potential disappointment.

Self-Doubt
Individuals who struggle with self-confidence or low self-esteem may doubt their ability to achieve meaningful goals. The fear of not measuring up to their own expectations or the expectations of others can undermine their motivation to set and pursue goals.

Preference for Flexibility
Some people thrive in environments with fewer constraints and prefer to maintain flexibility in their approach to work or life. These individuals may resist setting specific goals, fearing that doing so will limit their options or impede their adaptability to changing circumstances.

Understanding the factors that contribute to someone's aversion to setting goals sheds light on my prior boss's perspective in a way that is clearer than before. While I may not agree with him, it helped me gain perspective and understand the reasons behind his behavior. Leaders can also customize their approach to change management by understanding these factors of resistance and acknowledge common concerns. This approach helps create an environment conducive to successful goal setting and change implementation. At the end of the day, it all boils down to this - if you don't have goals, you won't know where you're going and if you don't know where you're going, you'll end up lost.

How does your organization currently utilize goal-setting frameworks like SMART goals, OKRs, or KPIs?

How would you rate your level of comfortability with using these frameworks in your own work or organizational context?

Encourage Reflection and Feedback

We already touched on how to effectively give feedback. Receiving feedback can be even more challenging though, especially for those in higher-up positions who are stuck on the myth that they need to know everything. It's like we've been wired to see feedback as a personal attack, something that threatens our self-worth or competence. Maybe it's because we've grown up in a culture that prizes unseizable perfection and sees admitting mistakes as a sign of weakness. Or perhaps it's because we've had bad experiences in the past, where feedback was delivered harshly or unfairly. Whatever the reason, the result is the same: we get defensive, argumentative, or even shut down when faced with feedback, even if it's meant to help us grow. But we need feedback to improve, both personally and professionally. So be honest with yourself here. How do you seek, process, and respond to feedback? Are you eager or is like a root canal? Wherever you are on the continuum, there are strategies to help navigate these situations without feeling offended or discouraged.

- Acknowledge that we all have insecurities, and no one is perfect, not even you. We are all just human.

- Recognize that it is probably difficult for the other person as well and respond in an empathetic manner.

- Approach feedback with an open mind and a growth mindset.

- Focus on specific behaviors they mention rather than the emotions you're feeling.

- Listen actively without becoming defensive when receiving feedback.

- Ask clarifying questions to ensure understanding.

- Express gratitude for the insights shared.

- View feedback as essential for growth and development, use what you want and appreciate the feedback you don't want.

Building on the foundation of personal development, the cultivation of a reflective practice and a culture of seeking out and responding well to constructive feedback emerges as indispensable components in fostering continuous growth and improvement. As previously acknowledged, personal development initiatives provide us with the tools and resources necessary to expand our skill sets and enhance our professional capabilities. However, the integration of reflection and feedback into this developmental journey amplifies its effectiveness, enabling us to gain deeper insights into our experiences and refine our skills with precision and purpose.

Reflection serves as a catalyst for self-discovery and self-awareness, prompting us to examine our thoughts, feelings, and actions in various contexts. By engaging in regular reflection on your experiences, you will extract valuable lessons and insights that inform your ongoing development, and you will open doors to others' needs as well. Whether through journaling, mindfulness practices, or structured reflection exercises, you can gain clarity and perspective on your strengths, weaknesses, and areas for growth, laying the groundwork for intentional and targeted skill development. In tandem with reflection, the solicitation and provision of feedback play a pivotal role in supporting growth and development.

Feedback serves as a mirror, reflecting back insights and observations that may not be immediately apparent. What's fascinating is that we all receive feedback differently. Some people are more inclined to hear and internalize negative feedback due to factors like perfectionism, low self-esteem, or a fear of failure. For them, negative feedback may reinforce existing self-doubts or insecurities, leading to heightened sensitivity to criticism. Conversely, others may have a natural inclination to focus on the positive aspects of feedback, perhaps due to a more optimistic outlook, a desire for affirmation, or a tendency to minimize shortcomings. These people may filter out or downplay negative feedback in favor of preserving a positive self-image or maintaining motivation. Additionally, confirmation biases can influence how feedback is interpreted. If someone expects criticism, they may be more likely to notice and remember negative feedback, while if they expect praise, they may selectively attend to positive feedback.

Overall, the tendency to hear only the negative or focus solely on the positive in feedback reflects the complex interplay of psychological, cognitive, and experiential factors that shape individuals' perceptions and responses. Recognizing and understanding these tendencies can help individuals develop greater self-awareness and resilience in processing feedback more effectively.

When leaders accept feedback well, individuals are more apt to seek feedback from peers, mentors, and supervisors, leveraging diverse perspectives to gain a comprehensive understanding of their performance and areas for improvement. This recognition of the individual journey, whether through models like Maslow's Hierarchy of Needs or the Kübler-Ross Change Curve, helps center us and cultivate empathy, fostering an environment where the emotion of sonder - acknowledging the complexities and experiences of others - becomes a guiding principle in our interactions and feedback exchanges.

Unfortunately, some leaders are feedback-adverse and lack self-awareness. As a result, they will often face significant setbacks in their personal and professional growth and can be very challenging to work with. Without it, leaders may remain unaware of their blind spots, limiting their ability to identify areas for improvement and make necessary adjustments to their behavior or leadership style. This can lead to stagnation or even regression in their leadership effectiveness over time.

Additionally, a lack of self-awareness can hinder a leader's ability to build strong relationships with their teams, as they may struggle to understand how their actions and decisions impact others. This can result in decreased trust, communication breakdowns, and ultimately, lower team morale and productivity. Furthermore, leaders who are resistant to feedback may be perceived as closed-minded or arrogant, which can damage their reputation and hinder their ability to effectively lead and inspire others. Overall, leaders who fail to embrace feedback and cultivate self-awareness are at risk of limiting their potential for growth and success in their roles.

Working with leaders who struggle to accept feedback and lack self-awareness can be quite challenging. And if you're not sure, look for some of the red flags: denying engagement in behaviors they frequently exhibit, resisting or becoming defensive when presented with feedback, and demonstrating an unwillingness to admit mistakes or take responsibility for failures. They may dismiss or ignore the perspectives of others, micromanage, lack empathy, and fail to adapt their leadership style to different situations or personalities, often claiming they don't change for anyone. Moreover, they tend to interact with a lack of transparency, demonstrating poor communication skills and maintaining a hierarchical rather than collaborative mindset.

Offering feedback to those who resist it is easier said than done, but there are ways to encourage them to be more open.

1. Approach the situation thoughtfully and strategically.

2. Start by highlighting specific examples of their behavior and its impact on the team or organization.

3. Use neutral language and avoid blaming or accusing tones.

4. Focus on solutions rather than problems.

5. Provide alternative approaches or examples of successful strategies.

6. Deliver the feedback in a private setting.

7. Choose an appropriate place and time.

8. Be prepared to listen actively and empathetically to the response.

9. Acknowledge their perspective and concerns. You may have been massaging your messaging for days, but this is the first they've heard of it.

10. Be open to further discussion or compromise.

It's important to acknowledge that not everyone is ready or willing to change, and that's okay. Some people may be comfortable with their current behaviors and resist any suggestion of change. While it's valuable to encourage growth and development, it's equally important to recognize that not everyone will be on the same journey towards change. Leaders who are resistant to change may have their reasons, whether it's fear of the unknown, past experiences, or simply a different set of priorities. And we can focus on our own growth and development without feeling the need to bring everyone along on our journey. Sometimes, leading by example and demonstrating the benefits of personal growth will simply inspire others to consider change in their own time and in their own way.

Reflect on your current attitude towards seeking and accepting feedback and how you have responded to it in the past.

How open are you to receiving constructive criticism and feedback from others, and what steps do you take to actively seek out opportunities for growth through feedback?

Invest in Personal Development

In the pursuit of unlocking individual potential, personal development emerges as a fundamental strategy for nurturing talent, fostering growth, and enhancing overall well-being. Recognizing the intrinsic value of self-improvement, the most successful organizations invest in personal development initiatives to empower their employees and drive organizational success.

Companies that prioritize personal development go beyond professional skill-building to support employees. They promote community outreach and service initiatives, where employees have opportunities to volunteer or engage in philanthropic activities, fostering a sense of social responsibility and belonging. They sponsor sports teams or wellness programs to promote physical health and camaraderie among employees. These initiatives encourage teamwork and collaboration and help individuals maintain a healthy work-life balance. Some of the best companies offer financial planning workshops, mental health resources, and even access to wellness retreats. These companies take a holistic approach to the work environment, rather than a fragmented one.

To aid in a holistic perspective, investing in personal development and wellbeing shouldn't solely fall on the shoulders of human resources though, as it often does. While HR plays a crucial role in facilitating training programs, providing resources, and promoting wellness initiatives, fostering personal growth and wellbeing is a shared responsibility across the organization. And investing in your own growth and development signifies a commitment to cultivating a culture of lifelong learning and self-improvement. When your team sees you working on self-improvement, chances are they will too. Whether it's learning a new language, participating in an exercise challenge or a book club, personal development initiatives offer you the chance to chart your own path towards professional fulfillment and success and model the same for others. By fostering a culture that values personal development, organizations not only attract top talent but also retain and engage their existing workforce, driving greater productivity, innovation, and overall success.

Consider your own approach to personal and professional development.

How do you currently prioritize your own growth and learning, and what steps do you take to invest in your development?

Invest in Leadership Development

Similar to personal development, leadership development is crucial for any organization aiming to prosper in today's market conditions. Considering that a Gallup study revealed that only 10% of the population naturally possess leadership qualities, while an additional 20% have the potential to excel as leaders with the right training and mentorship, investing in leadership development programs and mentorship opportunities becomes imperative. These initiatives are vital for cultivating individuals' potentials who might not initially demonstrate innate leadership traits. Through offering training, guidance, and support, organizations can expand their pool of effective leaders, thereby enhancing their ability to navigate change efficiently.

Whether for you or someone wanting to grow on your team, there are various ways to go about it. Several programs demonstrate an investment in leadership development, ranging from formal training initiatives to ongoing coaching and mentorship programs that can be conducted in-house or by hiring an outside consultant like The MindShift Effect. Some opportunities may include:

Leadership Training Workshops
Leadership training workshops provide foundational leadership skills and knowledge to emerging and established leaders. These workshops might address subjects like communication, decision-making, conflict resolution, and strategic thinking.

Executive Coaching
Executive coaching programs offer personalized support and guidance to senior leaders and executives. Coaches work one-on-one with leaders to help them identify strengths, address development areas, and achieve their professional goals via avenues like the Hogan Leadership Assessment.

Emerging Leader Programs
These are formal leadership development programs designed to cultivate the next generation of leaders within the company. These programs typically include a combination of training, mentoring, on-the-job experiences, and exposure to senior leadership.

Mentoring Programs
Mentoring programs pair employees with experienced mentors who can provide guidance, advice, and support as they navigate their careers. Mentors offer insights, share experiences, and help mentees develop key leadership competencies.

Leadership Conferences and Seminars
Attending leadership conferences, seminars, and industry events can provide leaders with valuable networking opportunities, exposure to new ideas, and insights from thought leaders in the field.

Leadership Retreats
Leadership retreats offer leaders a focused and immersive experience to reflect, recharge, and develop their leadership skills in a supportive environment. These retreats often include workshops, team-building activities, and opportunities for self-reflection.

Cross-Functional Rotations
Some organizations offer cross-functional rotation programs that allow leaders to gain exposure to different areas of the business and develop a broader understanding of organizational dynamics.

Online Learning Platforms
Online learning platforms offer a convenient and flexible way for leaders to access leadership development resources, including courses, webinars, articles, and videos on various leadership topics.

Investing in leadership development programs demonstrates a commitment to nurturing talent, fostering growth, and building a pipeline of capable leaders who can drive the organization forward in an ever-changing business landscape. Just like American author Tom Peters said, "Leaders don't create followers, they create more leaders", it's about unlocking potential, empowering individuals and teams to achieve their full capabilities, and make a meaningful impact in their personal and professional lives.

How does your company currently support the growth and development of its leaders?

Additionally, consider your own role in this process. Are you actively seeking out opportunities for leadership development, whether through formal training programs, coaching, or mentorship?

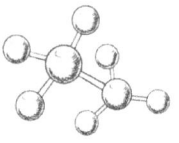

Part 5 Reflection

Reflecting on your organization's current approach to goal setting, which framework—OKRs, KPIs, or SMART goals—do you believe aligns most effectively with your organizational culture and objectives?

How might you tailor the implementation of this framework to maximize its benefits while mitigating potential drawbacks?

As a leader within your organization, how do you foster a culture that encourages open communication, reflection, and feedback among team members?

Considering your own professional development journey, identify one area in which you aim to invest for personal or professional growth. Outline a plan detailing specific actions you will take to pursue development in this area, including resources you will utilize, milestones you will set, and how you will measure progress.

PART 6: Strategic Planning

Strategic Framework

Every company, regardless of its size, location, or age, should possess a strategic framework—a set of shared beliefs that encompasses a vision, mission, core values, and strategy and every leader should be on board. These guiding principles, when integrated into the organization's operations, breathe life into its purpose and direction. Strategic frameworks:

Provide Clarity and Direction
A clear and compelling strategy provides clarity and direction for the organization, helping stakeholders understand where the organization is headed and how they can contribute to its success. A study published in the National Institutes of Health found that employees who have a clear understanding of their organization's goals and objectives are more likely to be engaged in their work and exhibit higher levels of job satisfaction.

Align Efforts and Resources
Strategic visioning aligns efforts and resources towards common goals and objectives, ensuring that everyone is working towards a shared vision and mission. According to a study by McKinsey & Company, teams that align their efforts and resources towards a common goal are nearly twice as likely to succeed than those that do not. When individuals and teams have a clear understanding of the overarching goal and how their contributions contribute to its attainment, they are more motivated and engaged in their work. People naturally gravitate towards shared goals because they provide a sense of purpose, belonging, and meaning, fostering collaboration and synergy among team members. This alignment not only enhances individual and team performance but also drives organizational success by harnessing collective efforts towards a common objective.

Neurologically, humans are wired to work towards common goals due to the inherent social nature of our species. Brain regions associated with social cognition and reward become active, reinforcing our desire for social bonds. Additionally, the mirror neuron system enables us to understand and empathize with others' experiences, fostering a sense of connection. Our brains release oxytocin, the hormone often referred to as the "love hormone" or "bonding hormone" fostering feelings of trust, empathy, cooperation, social bonding, and collective action. Dopamine is also activated when individuals work towards and achieve common goals, recognized as a reward. Consider the widespread followings of religions, nonprofit organizations, politics, and social movements. They all share a fundamental element: a unified strategic framework that brings together and resonates with its participants. This cohesion stems from our neurological responses, which reinforce behaviors linked to belonging to a larger community and connecting with others who share similar beliefs. Thus, from a neurological perspective, a strategic framework is necessary because it:

Inspire and Motivate

A compelling strategy inspires and motivates stakeholders to go above and beyond in pursuit of organizational goals. It creates a sense of purpose and meaning, driving engagement and commitment. Think about the greatest leaders throughout history. They have often been remembered for their ability to inspire and motivate others. These leaders possess a unique charisma and vision that captivates the hearts and minds of those around them, igniting a sense of purpose and passion within their followers. Whether it's through their powerful speeches, unwavering conviction, or leading by example, inspiring leaders have a profound impact on the people they lead. They have the remarkable ability to instill hope, courage, and determination in others, even in the face of adversity and have the ability to look down the road and strategically bring people along. By tapping into the deepest aspirations and values of their followers, these leaders inspire them to reach new heights, overcome obstacles, and achieve extraordinary feats. Ultimately, the legacy of inspiring leaders lives on in the hearts and minds of those they've touched, serving as inspiration for generations to come.

Help Guide Decision-Making

In today's fast-paced world, this cohesion serves as a distinct advantage for companies that can swiftly adapt while upholding shared values. A robust strategy acts as a beacon, guiding decision-making and ensuring alignment with the organization's overarching direction and principles. Research from the Harvard Business Review highlights this, revealing that organizations with a clear strategic vision are nearly 20% more likely to make decisions rapidly compared to those lacking a defined vision.

Foster Adaptability and Resilience

Having a strong strategy provides a framework for adaptability and resilience by offering a clear sense of direction and purpose amidst uncertainty and change. When leaders and organizations have a well-defined vision, they can anticipate potential challenges, identify emerging opportunities, and pivot as needed while staying aligned with their long-term goals. Moreover, it instills confidence and inspires commitment among team members, fostering a resilient culture where individuals are empowered to navigate obstacles, learn from setbacks, and innovate in the face of adversity.

Reflect on your organization's approach to strategic visioning. How does your company currently define and articulate its vision, mission, and values?

How would you rate the level of alignment between these guiding principles and the organization's goals and strategies?

Vision

A vision statement defines the desired future state or outcome that an organization aspires to achieve. It paints a picture of what success looks like and inspires and motivates stakeholders to work towards a common goal.

According to research conducted by Gallup, organizations with engaged employees who understand their company's vision and purpose experience a 240% boost in performance-related business outcomes compared to those with disengaged employees, where a vision is not visible. Another study published in the Journal of Applied Psychology found that companies with a strong vision are better equipped to navigate unforeseen challenges and disruptions in the business environment. This is because a well-defined vision serves as a compass, enabling leaders to stay focused on long-term objectives while remaining flexible in their approach to achieving them. Additionally, a vision promotes that shared sense of purpose and direction among employees, empowering them to adapt to changing circumstances and overcome obstacles with confidence.

Effective leaders understand the power of a compelling vision to inspire and motivate their teams toward innovation and change. By articulating a clear and compelling one, leaders provide a sense of direction and purpose, guiding their teams through periods of transformation. The vision should not only highlight the importance of innovation but also emphasize its connection to the organization's long-term success and relevance in a rapidly evolving market.

Moreover, leaders must communicate the vision effectively, ensuring that every member of the organization understands the significance of innovation and their role in driving change. By incorporating concepts like Simon Sinek's concept of "Start with Why," leaders can articulate the deeper purpose behind the vision, inspiring and motivating employees to embrace innovation wholeheartedly. When individuals comprehend the why behind their actions, they become more committed and engaged in achieving organizational goals, fostering a culture of creativity and forward-thinking within the company. By fostering a shared understanding of the vision and its implications, leaders can align their teams and galvanize collective action toward achieving innovative goals.

In addition to communicating the vision, leaders should actively involve their teams in shaping it, soliciting input and feedback to ensure buy-in and ownership. By empowering employees to contribute their ideas and perspectives, leaders foster a sense of ownership and commitment to the vision, increasing the likelihood of successful implementation. Through collaborative visioning processes, leaders can harness the collective intelligence and creativity of their teams, driving innovation and change from the ground up.

How well do you understand the process behind the creation of your company's vision?

What insights do you have regarding the development of the organizational vision, including who was involved, the methodologies used, and the overarching goals and values driving the visioning process?

Consider how this understanding influences your alignment with the company's long-term objectives and your role in contributing to its vision.

Mission

Mission and vision differ in their focus and scope within an organization. A vision statement outlines the desired future state or aspirations of the organization, describing what the organization ultimately aims to achieve or become. In contrast, a mission statement defines the organization's purpose, and primary objectives, outlining its reason for existence and how it intends to fulfill its goals. While a vision statement paints a picture of the ideal future, a mission statement focuses on the present activities and guiding principles that drive the organization towards that vision. It answers the question: "What do we do?" Writing a mission statement is a crucial step in defining the purpose and direction of your organization. Here are steps to guide you through the process:

1. **Define the purpose:** Clearly articulate the reason for the organization's existence and its fundamental objectives.

2. **Identify core values:** Determine the guiding principles and values that drive the organization's actions and decision-making.

3. **Consider stakeholders:** Consider the needs and expectations of various stakeholders, including employees, customers, shareholders, and the community.

4. **Assess strengths and capabilities:** Evaluate the organization's strengths, capabilities, and unique qualities that differentiate it from others.

5. **Draft the statement:** Use concise and impactful language to craft a statement that reflects the organization's purpose, values, and goals.

6. **Seek feedback:** Share the draft mission statement with stakeholders for input and feedback, ensuring that it resonates with the intended audience.

7. **Refine and finalize:** Incorporate feedback as needed and refine the mission statement until it accurately represents the organization's identity and aspirations.

8. **Communicate and integrate:** Once finalized, communicate the mission statement internally and externally, and integrate it into the organization's culture, strategy, and operations.

With these steps, crafting a mission statement that vividly outlines your organization's purpose and motivates stakeholders to unite behind its vision and objectives becomes achievable.

How meaningful and purposeful do you perceive your company's mission to be?

Does it effectively communicate the organization's purpose, and how well does it align with the company's actions and goals?

Does it serve its intended purpose of guiding decision-making and inspiring employees?

Values

Organizational values are the guiding principles and beliefs that define the organization's culture and behavior, and they should be more than just a poster on a wall. They should serve as a compass for decision-making and influence how individuals and teams interact and operate within the organization. Some tips for assessing or creating organizational values are:

1. **Assess Current Culture:** Begin by assessing the existing culture of your organization. Understand the prevailing norms, behaviors, and beliefs among employees. Identify both strengths and areas for improvement.

2. **Engage Stakeholders:** Engage key stakeholders, including employees, leaders, customers, and partners, in the values development process. Encourage open dialogue and collaboration to ensure diverse perspectives are considered.

3. **Brainstorm Values:** Conduct brainstorming sessions or workshops to generate ideas for values. Encourage participants to identify core principles and beliefs that are important to them and align with the organization's mission and goals.

4. **Prioritize and Define Values:** Review and prioritize the list of values generated during brainstorming. Identify common themes and shared priorities among stakeholders. Narrow down the list to a set of core values and clearly define each value to ensure shared understanding and alignment.

5. **Formalize and Embed Values:** Formalize the selected values into a cohesive set of guiding principles for the organization. Develop supporting materials, such as a values statement or code of conduct, to communicate the values effectively. Embed the values into all aspects of the

organization's culture and operations, ensuring they guide decision-making and behavior at every level.

With these steps, you can cultivate values that capture the essence of your organization, steer decision-making, and nurture a culture that is positive and purposeful. Developing organizational vision, mission, and values requires input from key stakeholders, including employees, customers, and other relevant stakeholders. It involves a process of reflection, dialogue, and consensus-building to identify and articulate the organization's core purpose, goals, and values.

Getting the right people involved in these conversations can be challenging though due to the delicate balance between inclusivity and efficiency. On one hand, including too many individuals in these discussions can lead to decision-making paralysis, diluted focus, and a lack of clarity. Conversely, excluding key stakeholders risks overlooking valuable perspectives, insights, and buy-in, which are essential for successful implementation. Achieving the optimal balance requires careful consideration of the relevance and impact of each participant's involvement, ensuring representation from diverse perspectives while maintaining a manageable group size conducive to productive dialogue and decision-making. Additionally, fostering a culture of openness, transparency, and inclusivity can encourage active participation and engagement from all stakeholders, regardless of their level or role within the organization. Although challenging, finding the right balance ensures that strategic discussions are enriched by diverse viewpoints while driving alignment, commitment, and collective ownership of the organization's direction and goals.

Balance also comes into play with timing. The frequency of reassessing or recreating a company's vision, mission, and core values varies depending on factors such as the company's growth stage, industry dynamics, and external market conditions. However, it's generally recommended that companies periodically review and, if necessary, update their vision, mission, and core values to ensure alignment with their current strategic objectives and evolving business environment.

For established companies, a comprehensive review of these elements may occur every few years, typically as part of a broader strategic planning process. This allows the company to reflect on its progress, assess changes in the market landscape, and adapt its direction and priorities accordingly. Additionally, major organizational changes such as mergers, acquisitions, or significant shifts in leadership may prompt a reassessment of the company's vision, mission, and core values.

For startups or rapidly growing companies, reassessing these elements may be more frequent, perhaps on an annual basis or even more frequently as the company scales and encounters new challenges or opportunities. In these cases, regular reviews help ensure that the company remains agile and responsive to changes in its competitive environment while maintaining clarity and alignment among its stakeholders.

Ultimately, the key is to strike a balance between stability and adaptability, ensuring that the company's vision, mission, and core values provide a guiding framework that is both enduring and responsive to the evolving needs of the business and its stakeholders.

How well do employees know and embody your company's values?

Are they actively promoted and reinforced by leadership or are they merely symbolic, displayed on posters without being genuinely embraced?

Strategy

Strategy is how the organization aims to realize its mission and vision, all while being guided by its core values. It serves as a comprehensive plan or roadmap, delineating the organization's objectives, goals, and methodologies for achieving them. I'll never forget my first trip to Dallas, Texas. If you have ever driven there, this may feel familiar to you. I had GPS in the car, and I heavily relied on it to navigate the city's insane highway system and rapid changes in traffic patterns. However, this proved to be too much for the GPS system, and it consistently lagged, leading me to miss so many exits and wrong turns. Here I had GPS, a roadmap of sorts, but couldn't depend on its reliability, and my brain experienced a mix of frustration, confusion, and stress. The discrepancy between having a tool, meant to provide direction, and its failure to do so triggered a sense of uncertainty and disorientation in me. After every missed exit and wrong turn, despite having GPS, my brain had to work overtime to process the situation, leading to increased cognitive load and emotional strain. And even though it wasn't Dallas's fault, I'll always associate the city with frustration, whether it's fair or not. My trip to Dallas taught me a valuable lesson: even with a roadmap, if it's not reliable, it's essentially useless.

A company strategy is no different. It's only as effective as the leaders who stand behind it and are aligned in unity. Just as a GPS relies on accurate input and coordinated direction to guide a journey, a company's strategy requires cohesive leadership to navigate the complexities of the business landscape. It steers decision-making and ensures efforts are aligned with long-term goals. When not executed or followed effectively, it inevitably leads to frustration, rebellion, or complete detachment from even the most dependable employees.

Practical Frameworks and Tools

Crafting and effectively communicating a captivating strategy, demands meticulous planning and execution, similar to implementing technology and systems to mitigate GPS lag. Once an organization firmly establishes these elements and integrates them into its culture, they become the guiding principles for all decisions, change initiatives, and projects within the company. Here are several practical frameworks and tools that may help:

SWOT Analysis
A SWOT (Strengths, Weaknesses, Opportunities, Threats) analysis will help you assess the organization's internal strengths and weaknesses and external opportunities and threats. You can use the insights gained from the analysis to inform the development of the vision, mission, and values.

Conducting a SWOT analysis offers several benefits for organizations and teams. It provides a structured framework for evaluating internal and external factors that can impact the organization's performance and strategic direction. By identifying strengths, organizations can leverage their competitive advantages and areas of excellence to capitalize on opportunities and mitigate threats. Conversely, recognizing weaknesses enables organizations to address areas for improvement and enhance their overall effectiveness.

Moreover, conducting a SWOT analysis facilitates strategic planning and decision-making by providing valuable insights into the organization's current position and prospects. It helps leaders prioritize initiatives, allocate resources efficiently, and develop action plans to address critical issues and capitalize on emerging opportunities. The process encourages cross-functional collaboration and communication, as stakeholders from various departments contribute their perspectives and expertise to the analysis.

A SWOT analysis fosters a proactive and forward-thinking mindset within the organization, enabling leaders to anticipate and adapt to changes in the business environment effectively. By identifying potential threats and emerging trends, organizations can develop contingency plans and strategic initiatives to mitigate risks and stay ahead of the competition.

Vision & Mission Workshops

Vision and mission workshops are collaborative and facilitated sessions aimed at defining or refining the vision and mission of an organization. During these workshops, participants, often including key stakeholders such as employees, leaders, and external partners, come together to discuss and explore the organization's aspirations, goals, values, and desired future state. Through various activities, exercises, and discussions, the workshop aims to elicit input, gather perspectives, and foster alignment. Facilitators guide the process, ensuring that the workshop remains focused, productive, and inclusive, ultimately leading to the development or enhancement of a clear and inspiring vision statement and mission for the organization.

Mission Statement Generator

A mission generator tool is a software application or online platform designed to assist organizations in creating or refining their mission statements. These tools typically provide a structured process and a series of prompts or questions to guide users through the development of a mission statement. Users input information about their organization, including its purpose, values, goals, and target audience, and the tool generates potential mission statement options based on this input. Mission generator tools may also offer features such as customization options, examples, and best practices to help users craft a mission statement that accurately reflects their organization's identity and objectives.

Values Assessment

Conduct a values assessment survey or workshop to identify and prioritize the organization's core values. Use techniques such as ranking exercises, group discussions, and storytelling to explore the significance of each value and how it aligns with the organization's mission and vision.

Communications Plan

Develop a comprehensive communications campaign to effectively communicate the vision, mission, and values to internal and external stakeholders. Use multiple channels and formats to educate, such as town hall meetings, intranet and website updates, newsletters, etc. to ensure broad reach, engagement, and adoption. Keeping messaging alive and consistent is also essential for maintaining organizational alignment. This is never a one-and-done event.

Reflect on your experience working with these frameworks and tools for strategic visioning?

What would you say your readiness and capacity is to apply these tools in future initiatives aimed at shaping the future direction of your organization.

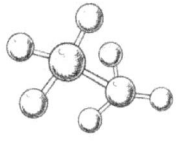

Part 6 Reflection

How can your understanding of the importance of clarity and direction in strategic visioning influence your approach to goal setting within your team or department?

Reflecting on the neurological mechanisms underlying collaboration towards common goals, how might you leverage this knowledge to foster greater teamwork and synergy within your organization?

How might you incorporate elements of inspiration and motivation into your own leadership style to empower your team towards achieving shared objectives?

PART 7: LEADING CHANGE

Leading Change

In the words of John F. Kennedy, "Change is the law of life. And those who look only to the past or present are certain to miss the future." Whether it involves integrating new technologies, reshaping organizational structures, or responding to market shifts, companies must adeptly navigate change to remain relevant and successful. A recent report from the Human Capital Institute highlighted that over the span of 2022-2023, a staggering 85% of organizations encountered difficulties with their change initiatives. Indeed, effectively guiding change demands a methodical strategy and meticulous preparation. Resistance, ambiguity, and apprehension about the future can impede progress and undermine well-conceived change efforts. So, let's dive into some essential insights on leading change.

Establish a Clear Vision and Purpose
Similar to a company vision, clearly define the vision and purpose of the change initiative, outlining the desired outcomes and benefits for the organization and its stakeholders. A compelling change vision provides direction and motivation, rallying support for the change effort.

Engage Stakeholders Early and Often
As with any significant initiative, engage key stakeholders throughout the change process, soliciting their input, addressing concerns, and building buy-in. Stakeholder engagement fosters ownership and commitment to the change initiative, increasing the likelihood of success.

Communicate Openly and Transparently
Communication is critical during times of change. Keep stakeholders informed and engaged through regular updates, town hall meetings, and other communication channels. Without over-communicating, be honest and transparent about the reasons for the change, its potential impact, and the expected outcomes. Finding the right balance in communication during change involves several key considerations:

Audience Needs
Understand the information needs and preferences of your stakeholders. Tailor your communication approach to meet these needs, whether it's providing detailed updates for some or high-level summaries for others.

Frequency
Determine an appropriate frequency for communication updates. Too much communication can lead to information overload, while too little can leave stakeholders feeling uninformed. Find a cadence that keeps stakeholders engaged without overwhelming them.

Clarity and Conciseness
Ensure your messages are clear, concise, and easy to understand. Avoid jargon and technical language and focus on conveying information in a straightforward manner.

Two-Way Communication
Establish avenues for two-way communication, enabling stakeholders to inquire, offer feedback, and express concerns. This fosters engagement and helps address any misunderstandings or issues that may arise.

Feedback Mechanisms
Implement feedback mechanisms to gauge stakeholder satisfaction with communication efforts. Regularly solicit feedback and adjust as needed to improve the effectiveness of communication.

By considering these factors and continuously evaluating and adjusting your communication approach, you will find the right balance that keeps stakeholders informed, engaged, and supportive throughout any change process without the risk of cognitive overload.

How would you describe your confidence level regarding your knowledge and skills in leading change and managing organizational transitions?

What have your experiences been like in leading change initiatives thus far?

Build a Coalition of Change Champions

Think about any impactful movement. While leaders may be at the forefront, a multitude of individuals play crucial roles in organizing, planning, and shaping the final outcome. Building a coalition of change champions is critical in any successful change initiative; a diverse group of individuals who can provide support, guidance, and advocacy throughout the change process. Prosci offers what they call the Stakeholder Analysis Matrix, which categorizes stakeholders into four groups: advocates, supporters, opponents, and observers. This framework provides a simplified, yet comprehensive overview of key stakeholders based on their level of influence and interest in the change initiative, aiding in targeted engagement strategies and effective change management. Let's walk through each stakeholder group and the roles they play.

Senior Leadership
According to Prosci's research, leadership sponsorship is consistently identified as the most critical success factor for change initiatives. In their "Best Practices in Change Management" research report, Prosci found that 96% of participants rated active and visible sponsorship by senior leaders as either important or very important for driving project and change success. This statistic underscores the pivotal role that leadership plays in driving change within organizations, emphasizing the need for leaders to actively champion and support change efforts for them to be successful.

Therefore, it's essential to engage senior leaders who can champion the change initiative from the top down. Their visible support and endorsement are critical for gaining organizational commitment and overcoming resistance to change. Senior leadership is often considered the most important group for driving change within an organization due to several key reasons:

Authority and Influence: Senior leaders hold positions of authority and influence within the organization. Their visible support and endorsement of the change initiative send a powerful message to employees, signaling that the change is a strategic priority for the organization.

Resource Allocation: Senior leaders control key resources, including budgetary allocations, staffing decisions, and strategic priorities. Their support is essential for allocating resources to support the change initiative, whether it involves funding for training programs, hiring additional staff, or investing in technology upgrades.

Organizational Culture: Senior leaders shape the organization's culture and values through their actions, decisions, and communication. By actively championing the change initiative, they can help create a culture that values innovation, adaptability, and continuous improvement, laying the foundation for successful change implementation.

Overcoming Resistance: Change initiatives often face resistance from employees who may be reluctant to embrace new ways of working or uncertain about the implications of the change. Senior leaders play a crucial role in overcoming resistance by addressing concerns, providing reassurance, and modeling the desired behaviors.

Strategic Alignment: Senior leaders are responsible for setting the organization's strategic direction and goals. Their involvement ensures that the change initiative is aligned with broader organizational objectives and priorities, increasing the likelihood of successful implementation and long-term sustainability.

Overall, senior leadership's active involvement and support are instrumental in driving change within an organization. Their commitment, influence, and strategic direction set the tone for the entire change initiative, inspiring confidence, mobilizing support, and ultimately leading to positive outcomes.

Middle Managers

Involve middle managers who play a crucial role in implementing and cascading the change within their respective teams. Empower them to act as change agents and provide them with the necessary resources and training to lead their teams effectively through the transition.

Frontline Employees

Include frontline employees who will be directly impacted by the change. Their input and participation are essential for understanding the practical implications of the change and identifying potential challenges or barriers to implementation.

Subject Matter Experts

Engage subject matter experts who possess the knowledge and expertise relevant to the change initiative. Their insights can help inform decision-making, shape implementation strategies, and address technical aspects of the change.

Cross-Functional Representatives

Include representatives from different departments or functional areas affected by the change. By involving cross-functional teams, you can ensure that diverse perspectives are considered, and potential interdepartmental issues are addressed proactively.

Change Agents

Identify and empower change agents—individuals who are enthusiastic, influential, and committed to driving the change forward. These individuals can serve as advocates, mentors, and role models for others, helping to inspire and mobilize support for the change initiative.

Key Stakeholders and Partners
Collaborate with key stakeholders, such as customers, suppliers, and external partners, who may have a vested interest in or be impacted by the change. Their involvement can help align the change initiative with broader organizational goals and ensure that external perspectives are considered.

Project Management Team
The synergy between project management and change management specialists is essential for the successful implementation of organizational initiatives. While project management focuses on the technical aspects of executing a project, such as timelines, budgets, and deliverables, change management addresses the human side of change, including employee engagement, resistance mitigation, communication, and adoption. By marrying these two disciplines, organizations can ensure that projects meet their objectives and achieve sustainable outcomes by effectively managing the people impacted by the change. This holistic approach integrates project execution with change implementation, resulting in smoother transitions, increased stakeholder engagement, and ultimately, greater project success.

In reality, successful change necessitates involvement and cooperation from every level of the organization, extending beyond executives in boardrooms. Utilizing the Stakeholder Analysis Quadrant during any change initiative can further help determine how to tailor messaging effectively at each stage, and involving the right people at the right time leads to more successful and sustainable outcomes.

Who do you believe should be identified as change champions within your organization, and why?

What criteria or characteristics do you think make individuals well-suited for this role, and how do you envision their involvement in driving change initiatives?

Align Change with Strategic Objectives

While I touched upon this earlier, it remains a crucial aspect often overlooked amidst the day-to-day operations. Aligning change initiatives with the organization's strategic objectives is paramount, similar to constructing a hierarchy of organizational needs, where each element supports and reinforces the next. By ensuring that change efforts are strategically aligned, organizations can prioritize initiatives that will have the most significant impact on overall performance and success. This strategic alignment helps to focus resources, prioritize activities, and ensure that change efforts are directed towards the areas that will drive the organization forward most effectively.

Strategy can be likened to a North Star guiding an organization through uncharted waters. Like a beacon in the night sky, a well-defined strategy provides direction and purpose, guiding decision making and actions toward a common destination. Just as sailors use the North Star to navigate the seas, organizations rely on their strategy to chart a course for success. However, simply having a strategy is not enough; everything else within the organization must align with this guiding star, including your change process. Every initiative, project, and decision should be evaluated against the strategic direction to ensure alignment and coherence. Like the stars in a constellation, each component of the organization should work together harmoniously, reinforcing the overarching strategy and driving the organization toward its desired future state. When everything aligns with the strategic North Star, organizations can navigate challenges with clarity and confidence, staying true to their purpose and vision.

What are your initial thoughts on how aligning change strategies with strategic objectives can impact organizational success?

How do you envision this alignment influencing the outcome of change initiatives within your organization?

Invest in Change Management Capabilities

Change management as a formal discipline has greatly evolved over time. While the concept of managing change has existed for centuries, it wasn't until the mid-20th century that it began to gain traction as a structured approach within organizations. One early influential figure in change management was Kurt Lewin, a psychologist who introduced the concept of the "unfreezing-change-refreezing" model in the 1940s. Lewin emphasized the importance of understanding the psychology of individuals and groups when implementing change. In the 1980s and 1990s, with the rise of globalization and rapid technological advancements, organizations faced increasing pressure to adapt to change quickly. This led to a growing recognition of the need for formal change management practices to address resistance and facilitate successful transitions.

In the late 20th and early 21st centuries, change management became more widely recognized as a critical organizational competency. Numerous methodologies and frameworks emerged, such as John Kotter's 8-Step Process for Leading Change and Prosci's ADKAR model, providing structured approaches for managing change initiatives. Today, change management is an integral part of organizational strategy, with dedicated professionals and consultants specializing in guiding organizations through complex transformations.

Though the principles of change management have existed for decades, its formalization and widespread adoption as a discipline have emerged relatively recently in organizational history. Many organizations still grapple with understanding its function and benefits, underscoring the critical need to equip both leaders and employees with the necessary skills and knowledge to navigate change effectively. Here are several strategies for investing in change management capabilities:

Training and Development
Provide training programs and workshops to equip employees, managers, and leaders with the knowledge and skills needed to effectively manage change. This training may cover topics such as change management principles, communication strategies, stakeholder engagement, and resistance management.

Certifications and Qualifications
Encourage employees to pursue certifications and qualifications in change management. Organizations like Prosci offer certification classes for change managers, specialists, and practitioners. These certifications provide individuals with a recognized credential and demonstrate their expertise in managing change.

Internal Change Management Teams
Establish internal change management teams or departments tasked with leading and supporting change initiatives across the organization. These teams can provide expertise, structure, guidance, and resources to project teams and business units undertaking change efforts.

External Consultants and Experts
Seek support from external change management consultants or experts, like the MindShift Effect, who can provide specialized knowledge, experience, and resources to support specific change initiatives. These consultants can offer valuable insights, best practices, and support throughout the change process.

Technology and Tools
Invest in change management technology and tools to streamline and enhance change management processes. This may include project management software, communication platforms, collaboration tools, and analytics solutions designed to support change planning, execution, and evaluation.

Continuous Improvement
Foster a culture of continuous improvement by regularly evaluating and refining change management practices and processes. Encourage feedback from employees and stakeholders

involved in change initiatives, and use insights gained to enhance future change efforts.

Change Leadership Development
Develop change leadership capabilities among senior leaders and managers to ensure they have the skills and competencies needed to effectively lead change efforts. This may involve leadership development programs, coaching, and mentoring focused on change leadership skills.

By investing in change management capabilities, organizations can build the resilience, agility, and capacity needed to navigate change successfully and achieve their strategic objectives. Just as we've come to recognize the value that structured project management offers, a similar appreciation is beginning to emerge for change management. However, like any new concept, it will require time to fully unfold and integrate into organizational practices.

What's your understanding of change management capabilities, and how does your company currently invest in developing or leveraging them?

Manage Resistance and Overcome Barriers

Whenever you introduce new concepts, methods, and ways of thinking, you're bound to encounter resistance. Go back to concepts we hit on earlier - when faced with something unfamiliar and new, our brains often activate the amygdala, which can trigger feelings of discomfort and caution. Additionally, the prefrontal cortex may engage to assess the situation and determine how to respond, both positively and negatively. So, anticipate resistance because it will happen. Here are some effective strategies to manage it when it does happen:

Education and Training
Provide education and training to help employees understand the rationale behind the change and how it aligns with organizational goals. Offer workshops, seminars, or informational sessions to equip employees with the knowledge and skills needed to adapt to the change effectively. By empowering employees with information and resources, you can mitigate resistance stemming from uncertainty or lack of understanding.

Engagement and Involvement
As mentioned before, involve employees in the change process by soliciting their input, involving them in decision-making, and delegating responsibilities where appropriate. By actively engaging employees in the change initiative, you foster a sense of ownership and commitment, reducing resistance and increasing buy-in. Encourage participation in cross-functional teams or working groups tasked with driving specific aspects of the change.

Address Concerns Proactively
Proactively address concerns and objections raised by employees regarding the change. Take the time to listen to their perspectives, acknowledge their concerns, and provide reassurance where possible. Offer support mechanisms, such as mentorship programs or employee assistance programs, to help individuals cope with the challenges associated with change. By

demonstrating empathy and understanding, you can build trust and mitigate resistance.

Celebrate Successes and Milestones
Ignite the dopamine. Recognize and celebrate successes and milestones achieved throughout the change process. Acknowledge the efforts of employees who have embraced the change and contributed to its success. Celebrating achievements helps boost morale, reinforces positive behaviors, and motivates employees to continue supporting the change initiative.

Resist the Urge to Make Assumptions
Making assumptions can be detrimental when trying to overcome resistance and barriers to change. Even if you've been deeply involved in an initiative for months and are enthusiastic about its prospects, assuming that everyone else will share your excitement and immediately embrace the change is unrealistic. People have different perspectives, experiences, and concerns that may not align with yours. By making assumptions, you risk overlooking valid objections, concerns, or resistance from stakeholders, which can undermine the success of the change initiative.

Picture a runner at the front of the Boston Marathon, prepared to sprint when the starting gun fires, while those at the back are unaware the race has even begun. This analogy beautifully reflects the dynamics of change management - how assumptions about readiness for change can lead to disparities in understanding and engagement. Just as the runner at the front is poised to move forward while others may not even be aware of the race starting, in change management, assuming everyone is prepared when you are can result in miscommunication, resistance, or disengagement from those who haven't been adequately informed or involved in the process.

What structures or processes, if any, does your organization have in place to manage resistance and overcome barriers during periods of change?

If so, how effectively are they utilized?

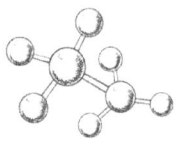

Part 7 Reflection

How do you plan to apply the principles of establishing a clear vision and purpose, engaging stakeholders early and often, and communicating openly and transparently to drive successful change initiatives within your organization?

Reflecting on the importance of empowering employees and building a coalition of change champions, what specific steps will you take to foster a culture of empowerment and advocacy for change within your team?

Considering the alignment of change strategies with strategic objectives and investment in change management capabilities, what initiatives can you lead or support to ensure that change efforts are strategically aligned, well-executed, and effectively managed within your organization?

PART 8 - YOUR CHEAT SHEET TO CHANGE MODELS, THEORIES, AND APPROACHES

As you engage with the content of this chapter, take a moment to envision how you, in your role as a leader, might engage with the different change models presented. Reflect on whether you've observed any of these models being utilized within your organization and consider their alignment with its culture, goals, and challenges. This introspection can provide valuable insights into how you can leverage this knowledge to inform your own decision-making processes and guide strategic planning efforts aimed at driving meaningful change.

As you explore each model and theory, approach them with a critical lens, evaluating their practical applications and implications for your unique leadership style and approach. By actively engaging with this information, you'll be better equipped to navigate complex change initiatives, inspire your team, and ultimately achieve transformative outcomes. Effective change leadership requires a multifaceted approach that draws upon various models, theories, and methodologies. Now, we will embark on a journey to break down these change models, theories, and approaches in detail. Understanding the nuances of these frameworks is crucial for several reasons:

Toolkit for change
They provide a toolkit to navigate the complexities of change management, allowing you to tailor your strategies to different organizational contexts and challenges.

Organizational Dynamics
They may help foster a deeper understanding of the underlying principles and dynamics of organizational change, empowering you to make informed decisions and anticipate potential obstacles.

Critical Thinking
These theories foster critical thinking and creativity, encouraging you to explore innovative solutions and adapt your approaches to ever-evolving circumstances.

All change management models share several common elements, despite their differences in approach and methodology. They all highlight the need for:

- A structured process to guide organizations through periods of change. This typically involves stages or phases that help leaders plan, implement, and sustain change initiatives effectively.
- Stakeholder engagement and communication. Great leaders understand that involving employees, customers, and other key stakeholders in the change process is essential for building buy-in, fostering ownership, and driving successful outcomes.
- Strong leadership and effective governance throughout the change journey. Great leaders recognize their role in setting the tone, establishing the vision, and providing direction and support to their teams during times of change. They understand that their actions and behaviors significantly influence how change is perceived and embraced within the organization.
- Flexibility and adaptability in response to evolving circumstances. Great leaders know that change is dynamic and unpredictable, requiring them to be agile and responsive to emerging challenges and opportunities. They understand the need to continuously assess progress, adjust strategies as needed, and cultivate a culture of learning and innovation.

Ultimately, great leaders understand that change management models are valuable tools that provide frameworks and guidelines for navigating change effectively. While each model may offer different approaches and techniques, the fundamental principles of effective change leadership remain consistent. By embracing these principles and leveraging the insights from various change management models, you can enhance your own ability to lead successful change initiatives and drive organizational transformation.

Prosci's Model & Methodology

The Prosci program encompasses a comprehensive approach to change management, far beyond what is outlined here. However, the aim here is to provide a brief overview for means of comparison. Prosci's ADKAR model is a popular framework for understanding individual change and guiding change management efforts within organizations overview as a starting point for comparing different methodologies.

The acronym **ADKAR** stands for:

A - Awareness of the need for change
This stage involves understanding why change is necessary and recognizing the implications of not changing. Individuals must comprehend the reasons behind the change and its potential impact on them personally and professionally.

D - Desire to participate and support the change
Once individuals are aware of the need for change, they must develop a desire to support and engage in the change process. This stage focuses on building motivation and commitment to the change initiative. Change initiatives frequently stall or encounter obstacles in this phase, where individuals may struggle to fully embrace or commit to the proposed changes. This phase is critical for cultivating motivation and enthusiasm for the change, and addressing barriers such as uncertainty, fear, or resistance can help propel the initiative forward.

K - Knowledge of how to change
Individuals need the necessary knowledge and skills to effectively participate in the change. This stage involves providing training, resources, and support to help individuals develop the competencies required to adapt to the new way of working.

A - Ability to implement required skills and behaviors
With the knowledge and skills in place, individuals must demonstrate the ability to implement the required changes in their day-to-day work. This stage focuses on supporting employees as they apply new behaviors, processes, and tools in their roles.

R - Reinforcement to sustain the change
Finally, sustaining change requires ongoing reinforcement and support. This stage involves recognizing and rewarding desired behaviors, providing feedback and coaching, and adjusting systems and processes to reinforce the change over time.

Prosci's approach to change management is based on the understanding that successful change occurs when individuals within the organization adopt and embrace the change. Their methodology emphasizes the importance of addressing the people side of change alongside the technical aspects of the initiative. Prosci's change management methodology provides a structured approach for managing change initiatives, including:

Change Readiness: Conducting change readiness assessments to identify potential barriers and challenges.

Communicating: Developing comprehensive communication and stakeholder engagement plans.

Training: Offering training and assistance to aid employees in adjusting to new work methodologies.

Monitoring: Monitoring progress and adjusting strategies as needed to ensure successful implementation.

Celebrating: Celebrating successes and recognizing the contributions of individuals and teams throughout the change process.

Prosci's model and methodologies offer organizations a structured approach to managing change, providing a clear and systematic framework for navigating complex transformation initiatives. By emphasizing the human side of change, Prosci's model helps organizations understand and address resistance among employees, fostering greater acceptance and adoption of new processes or systems. Grounded in extensive research and best practices, Prosci's methodologies enable data-driven decision-making, allowing organizations to track progress, identify areas for improvement, and refine their change strategies accordingly.

However, there are also some drawbacks to consider. The model's focus on linear processes may not always align with the dynamic and complex nature of organizational change, potentially limiting its adaptability to evolving circumstances. The rigidity of the model could hinder organizational agility and flexibility, particularly in fast-paced environments where rapid adjustments are necessary. Its narrow focus on individual and team-level change may overlook broader systemic issues within the organization, such as structural or cultural barriers that could impede successful change implementation. Furthermore, surface-level solutions generated by the model may fail to address underlying root causes of resistance or inefficiencies, necessitating a deeper understanding of organizational dynamics. While Prosci's model offers valuable tools and methodologies, organizations should approach its implementation with a critical eye, considering its suitability for their specific context and needs.

Lewin's Change Management Model

Lewin's Change Management Model, developed by psychologist Kurt Lewin in the 1940s, remains one of the most influential frameworks for understanding and managing organizational change. The model consists of three key stages: unfreezing, changing, and refreezing.

Unfreezing: This initial stage involves preparing the organization for change by breaking down existing mindsets, behaviors, and structures. Leaders must create a sense of dissatisfaction with the current situation and establish a compelling case for change. Strategies for unfreezing may include communication, education, and involvement to help stakeholders understand the need for change and overcome resistance.

Changing: Once the organization is unfrozen, the focus shifts to implementing the desired changes. This stage involves introducing new processes, systems, behaviors, or structures aimed at achieving the desired outcomes. Effective communication, leadership support, and employee engagement are critical during this phase to ensure that the change is embraced and implemented successfully.

Refreezing: In the final stage, the changes are institutionalized and integrated into the organization's culture and practices. Refreezing involves reinforcing the new behaviors and processes, providing support and training as needed, and celebrating successes. By solidifying the changes, leaders can ensure that they become the new norm and are sustained over the long term.

Lewin's model is valuable because it emphasizes the importance of managing the transition process and acknowledges that change involves both individual and organizational dynamics. It provides a structured framework for leaders to plan and execute change initiatives effectively while addressing resistance and promoting employee buy-in. However, it's important to note that organizations today often face more complex and dynamic change environments than those envisioned by Lewin, necessitating the integration of additional change management approaches and methodologies.

Kotter's 8-Step Change Model

Kotter's 8-Step Change Model is a comprehensive framework for leading organizational change effectively. Crafted by Harvard Business School professor John Kotter during the 1990s, this framework offers a systematic method for overseeing change endeavors. The eight steps are as follows:

1. **Establish a Sense of Urgency:** Kotter emphasizes the importance of creating a compelling reason for change by highlighting the urgency of the situation. Leaders must communicate the need for change and the consequences of inaction to motivate stakeholders to support the initiative.

2. **Form a Powerful Coalition:** Successful change requires strong leadership and a dedicated team of change agents. Leaders should assemble a coalition of key stakeholders who have the authority, expertise, and influence to drive the change process forward.

3. **Create a Vision for Change:** Leaders must articulate a clear and inspiring vision that outlines the desired future state of the organization. The vision should be concise, compelling, and aligned with the organization's values and strategic objectives.

4. **Communicate the Vision:** Effective communication is essential for gaining buy-in and commitment from stakeholders. Leaders should consistently communicate the vision for change through various channels and engage employees at all levels of the organization.

5. **Empower Broad-Based Action:** To implement the vision, leaders must empower employees to take ownership of the change process and contribute their ideas and efforts. This includes eliminating obstacles, allocating resources, and

nurturing an environment that promotes collaboration and innovation.

6. **Generate Short-Term Wins:** Celebrating quick wins and milestones helps maintain momentum and builds confidence in the change initiative. Leaders should identify opportunities for early successes and recognize and reward progress along the way.

7. **Consolidate Gains and Produce More Change:** Building on initial successes, leaders should continue to drive progress toward the vision by addressing remaining challenges and obstacles. This may involve refining processes, addressing resistance, and scaling up successful initiatives.

8. **Anchor New Approaches in the Culture:** Sustainable change requires embedding new behaviors and practices into the organization's culture. Leaders should ensure that the changes are institutionalized through policies, systems, and structures that support the desired outcomes.

Kotter's 8-Step Model offers valuable advantages for managing change within organizations. Its clear and structured framework provides a roadmap, guiding stakeholders through each phase of the change process. By focusing on creating a sense of urgency, the model helps to mobilize stakeholders and overcome resistance, while emphasizing communication and empowerment fosters engagement and buy-in, critical for successful implementation. The sequential nature of the steps offers a logical progression, aiding in the management of complex change initiatives. Widely recognized and extensively used, the model enjoys broad acceptance in the field of organizational change management.

However, Kotter's model also has its limitations. Its linear approach may not always align with the dynamic and nonlinear nature of change, potentially hindering adaptability. Moreover, the heavy reliance on leadership throughout the process may limit scalability and long-term sustainability. The model's lack of emphasis on employee involvement and feedback could contribute to resistance and undermine the success of change efforts. Additionally, it provides limited guidance on addressing cultural and behavioral aspects of change, which are often integral to successful implementation. Finally, the implementation of Kotter's 8-Step Model may be time-consuming and resource-intensive, requiring significant investment from organizations.

While Kotter's 8-step model offers a valuable framework for change management, organizations should complement it with additional methodologies and strategies to address the multifaceted challenges of organizational change effectively while recognizing its required investment.

McKinsey 7-S Framework

The McKinsey 7-S Framework is a management model developed by consulting firm McKinsey & Company in the 1980s. It provides a holistic approach to organizational effectiveness by focusing on seven interdependent elements that are crucial for organizational success. The seven elements are:

1. **Strategy:** This denotes the plan of action devised by the organization to accomplish its objectives and goals. It encompasses decisions about what the organization will do and how it will allocate resources to achieve its desired outcomes.

2. **Structure:** Structure refers to the hierarchical organization of roles, responsibilities, and reporting relationships within the organization. It includes both formal and informal aspects of organizational design and governance.

3. **Systems:** Systems comprise the processes, procedures, and routines that regulate how tasks are carried out within the organization. This encompasses everything from decision-making processes to performance management systems and information technology infrastructure.

4. **Shared Values:** Shared values represent the organization's core beliefs, principles, and culture. They guide behavior and decision-making within the organization and shape its identity and reputation.

5. **Skills:** Skills refer to the capabilities and competencies of the organization's workforce. This includes both technical skills related to specific tasks and roles, as well as softer skills such as communication, leadership, and problem-solving.

6. **Style:** Style refers to the leadership style and management practices employed within the organization. It encompasses the behavior and attitudes of senior leaders, as well as the overall organizational culture.

7. **Staff:** Staff refers to the organization's workforce, including employees at all levels and in all functions. It involves considerations such as recruitment, training, development, and retention of talent.

The McKinsey 7-S Framework emphasizes the interconnectedness of these seven elements and suggests that they must be aligned and mutually reinforcing for the organization to be effective. It is often used as a diagnostic tool to assess the current state of an organization and identify areas for improvement or change. By addressing any misalignments or gaps between the seven elements, organizations can enhance their overall performance and achieve their strategic objectives.

While the McKinsey 7-S framework offers a comprehensive approach to organizational analysis and change, it also comes with its share of drawbacks. One significant challenge is its complexity, as the framework involves seven interrelated elements that must be addressed simultaneously, making it potentially daunting for organizations to implement effectively. Additionally, the abstract nature of some components, such as shared values and skills, can lead to ambiguity in how they should be defined and measured, further complicating the implementation process. Moreover, the framework's limited focus on external factors may pose challenges, as it overlooks crucial aspects such as market dynamics, competitive landscape, and regulatory environment, which are vital for organizational success. This oversight could potentially hinder organizations from effectively responding to external changes and disruptions, ultimately impacting their ability to thrive in a dynamic environment.

Agile Change Management

Agile Change Management is an approach that applies the principles of Agile methodology to the process of managing organizational change. Agile, originally developed for software development, emphasizes iterative, incremental, and flexible approaches to project management. If you're familiar with Agile in project management, you'll recognize that it shares the same principles of adaptability, collaboration, and iterative development. When applied to change management, Agile principles can help organizations navigate complex and dynamic environments more effectively. Here are some key characteristics and principles of Agile Change Management:

Iterative Approach
Agile Change Management involves breaking down change initiatives into smaller, manageable increments or iterations. Instead of implementing changes all at once, organizations make incremental progress, allowing for continuous feedback and adaptation along the way.

Flexibility and Adaptability
Agile Change Management emphasizes the ability to respond to change quickly and effectively. It recognizes that change is inevitable and that organizations must be able to adapt their plans and strategies in response to new information or shifting priorities.

Stakeholder Collaboration
Agile Change Management emphasizes collaboration and engagement with stakeholders throughout the change process. By involving key stakeholders early and often, organizations can gain valuable insights, build buy-in, and address concerns more effectively.

Empirical Learning
Agile Change Management encourages a culture of continuous learning and improvement. Organizations gather feedback from stakeholders and evaluate the effectiveness of change initiatives through empirical data, allowing them to make data-driven decisions and adjust their approach as needed.

Transparency and Communication
Agile Change Management promotes transparency and open communication within the organization. By providing visibility into the change process and progress, organizations can build trust, manage expectations, and foster a supportive environment for change.

Cross-Functional Teams
Agile Change Management often involves forming cross-functional teams that bring together individuals with diverse skills and perspectives. These teams work collaboratively to drive change initiatives forward, leveraging their collective expertise and experience.

Rapid Prototyping and Experimentation
Agile Change Management encourages organizations to test ideas and solutions through rapid prototyping and experimentation. By taking a lean, iterative approach, organizations can quickly validate assumptions, identify potential issues, and refine their approach based on real-world feedback.

Agile Change Management allows organizations to quickly respond to changing circumstances and evolving stakeholder needs, enabling them to stay relevant and competitive in dynamic environments. The iterative nature of it encourages continuous collaboration and feedback from stakeholders throughout the change process, fostering a sense of ownership and buy-in. By breaking down change initiatives into smaller, manageable increments or sprints, the process facilitates incremental progress and allows organizations to course-correct based on real-time feedback, reducing the risk of large-scale project failures.

However, it also presents challenges. The complexity inherent in Agile methodologies can overwhelm organizations not accustomed to iterative approaches, potentially leading to resistance and confusion among stakeholders. Additionally, the rapid pace of change and uncertainty associated with Agile can pose difficulties in planning and maintaining alignment with strategic objectives. Despite these drawbacks, organizations can mitigate these challenges through effective leadership, clear communication, and ongoing stakeholder engagement throughout the change process.

Appreciative Inquiry

Appreciative Inquiry (AI) is a strengths-based approach to organizational development and change management that focuses on identifying and amplifying what is working well within an organization. Developed by David Cooperrider and his colleagues in the 1980s, AI is grounded in the belief that organizations grow and evolve in the direction of the questions they ask and the stories they tell about themselves. The key principles of Appreciative Inquiry include:

Positive Core
AI starts by identifying and amplifying the positive core of an organization—the strengths, successes, and moments of excellence. By focusing on what is already working well, AI aims to build on these positive aspects to drive change and transformation.

Inquiry and Dialogue
AI uses a process of inquiry and dialogue to explore the positive core of an organization. This involves asking open-ended questions that encourage reflection, storytelling, and sharing of experiences. Through meaningful conversations, participants gain new insights, perspectives, and ideas for action.

Co-Creation
AI emphasizes the importance of co-creating the future of the organization through collaborative dialogue and engagement. By involving a diverse range of stakeholders in the change process, AI fosters a sense of ownership, commitment, and collective responsibility for driving change.

Appreciative Learning
AI views learning as a continuous and generative process that emerges from appreciative inquiry and dialogue. By reflecting on past successes and exploring possibilities for the future,

organizations can learn from their experiences and adapt their strategies accordingly.

Sustainable Change
AI aims to create sustainable change by building on the strengths and capabilities of the organization. Rather than focusing on fixing problems or deficits, it encourages organizations to leverage their existing assets to achieve their desired outcomes and aspirations. Appreciative Inquiry typically follows a four-phase process known as the 4-D Cycle:

1. **Discovery**
   In this phase, participants explore and appreciate the best of what currently exists within the organization. This involves identifying past successes, core values, and positive experiences that can serve as a foundation for future change.

2. **Dream**
   Participants envision and articulate a compelling and inspiring future for the organization. This phase encourages creativity, imagination, and aspirational thinking, allowing participants to dream big and explore new possibilities.

3. **Design**
   In the design phase, participants co-create strategies, initiatives, and action plans to bring their vision to life. This involves identifying concrete steps, setting goals, and developing implementation plans that align with the organization's values and aspirations.

4. **Destiny (or Delivery)**
   The final phase involves implementing and sustaining the changes identified in the design phase. Participants take action, monitor progress, and celebrate achievements as they work towards realizing their shared vision for the future.

Appreciative Inquiry stands out for its ability to catalyze positive change within organizations by leveraging strengths, successes, and positive experiences as catalysts for transformation. One of its primary benefits lies in its positive focus, which creates an optimistic and energizing atmosphere conducive to innovation and collaboration. By encouraging stakeholders to reflect on past successes and moments of peak performance, AI fosters a sense of empowerment and motivation, driving individuals to envision and co-create a desired future together. This approach not only inspires confidence and optimism but also cultivates a shared sense of purpose and commitment among participants, laying the groundwork for sustainable organizational change.

However, despite its strengths, it may present some drawbacks that organizations need to consider. One such drawback is its potential to overlook or downplay existing challenges and problems within the organization due to its emphasis on positivity. This bias towards positivity may hinder the organization's ability to confront and address critical issues effectively, leading to missed opportunities for improvement. Additionally, the focus on idealized visions of the future may create unrealistic expectations or goals that are challenging to achieve, potentially resulting in disappointment or disillusionment if objectives are not met. It is crucial for organizations to balance the positive focus of Appreciative Inquiry with a realistic assessment of challenges and limitations to ensure that change initiatives are both inspiring and practical.

Exposure to different models cultivates critical thinking skills, promotes innovation in leadership approaches, and enhances cultural competence. Ultimately, I hope this knowledge equips you with the tools and insights needed to navigate complex change initiatives successfully, fostering organizational resilience and growth.

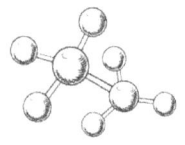

Part 8 Reflection

How prevalent is the language and terminology associated with various change management theories and programs in your organization?

Imagine you're leading a major change project in your organization. How would you tailor your change management strategy to incorporate elements from different change methodologies, ensuring a comprehensive approach to addressing resistance and driving successful implementation?

How might you incorporate diverse change management frameworks into your leadership approach to promote a culture of continuous improvement and adaptability within your organization?

CONCLUSION: EMBRACE THE MINDSHIFT EFFECT

Change management and leadership development represent more than just organizational strategies – they embody a profound shift in mindset and approach. It's about recognizing that to impact meaningful change in our organizations, we must first look inward, confronting our own limitations, perspectives, biases, and fears. By doing the internal work, we become catalysts for transformation, inspiring others through our example and empowering them to reach their full potential.

As leaders, we can create environments where authenticity, empathy, and growth are valued, leading to stronger, more resilient organizations and happier, more fulfilled employees. It's a journey of self-discovery and empowerment, and by embracing it wholeheartedly, we pave the way for a brighter future for ourselves and those we lead.

Embrace the idea that mindset shifts are the cornerstone for your personal and professional growth. Challenge your limiting beliefs, adopt new perspectives, and foster a growth mindset to unlock your full potential and achieve remarkable feats.

Recognize the importance of leadership development and understand that effective leadership is vital for driving change, fostering innovation, and motivating others to reach their highest potential. Commit to continuous growth and development and embrace the concept that personal and professional growth is an ongoing journey. Adopt a mindset of continuous learning, adaptation, and improvement to stay ahead of the curve, seize opportunities for growth, and lead with impact in an ever-changing world.

Manage change with confidence and acknowledge that change is inevitable in today's dynamic business environment but understand that you can navigate it with confidence. Implement strategic change management approaches, prioritize stakeholder engagement, communication, and resilience to effectively manage and adapt to change.

Foster connections through empathy and authenticity and realize the power of both in building trust and collaboration within your teams and organizations. Lead with empathy, authenticity, and humility to create inclusive cultures that drive innovation and high performance.

My greatest hope is that The MindShift Effect has inspired you to challenge conventional thinking and explore new possibilities for driving organizational transformation. Throughout our journey, we've explored the pivotal role of leadership in shaping organizational culture and propelling change from within, emphasizing the importance of leading by example and embodying resilience, agility, and a commitment to continuous improvement.

Moreover, The MindShift Effect highlights the value of integrating insights from various change management models and approaches. By blending these insights with the principles outlined in this book, I hope you have enhanced your capacity to navigate complex change initiatives and inspire others to embrace new ways of working. Now, take some to time consider some final questions on the next page to establish your mindset.

Final Reflection

What kind of mindset shift has taken place for you after understanding the neuropsychology of change, and how might it influence your approach to leadership?

As you apply the principles of leading by example and empowering others in driving change, how might these transformations in perspective shape your vision for catalyzing positive transformation in future endeavors?

Considering the refinement of your communication skills, how will these changes in interactions and connections with others empower you to build trust and understanding in future collaborations?

With strategic visioning and change management frameworks in mind, how do you foresee these shifts in approach guiding your future navigation of uncertainty and goal achievement, and how might they align with your evolving personal and organizational aspirations?

Remember, the journey of personal and professional growth is a lifelong pursuit. Embrace The MindShift Effect, lead with impact, and empower others to do the same. Together, we can create a world where everyone can reach their full potential and make a positive difference in the lives of others. It is an ongoing process, and embracing both areas of strength and areas for improvement is essential for personal and professional growth. Incorporating the insights gained from reading this into your own leadership approach can pave the way for greater effectiveness and success. By leveraging the power of The MindShift Effect, you can continue to refine your leadership skills, drive positive change, and inspire those around you to reach their full potential.

While some aspects of leadership development and change management might appear straightforward to an observer, you and I recognize that it's far from simple. Being a stellar leader and adept change manager involves grasping and applying psychological theories and methodologies, as well as appreciating neuropsychology behind human behavior and reactions in different situations. To be a great leader, you must be willing to embrace the discomfort, for it is often the crucible in which true growth and transformation occur.

The hard work of introspection, self-awareness, and personal development may feel daunting, but it is precisely through these challenges that we unlock our greatest potential. By confronting our fears, biases, and limitations head-on, we open the door to new possibilities and opportunities for growth. So, don't shy away from the discomfort – lean into it, for on the other side lies the path to becoming the best version of yourself and achieving extraordinary outcomes! As British philosopher Alan Watts once said, "The only way to make sense out of change is to plunge into it, move with it, and join the dance."

Let's keep dancing together.

For more information on The
MindShift Effect and explore
leadership development and
change management coaching
and consulting,
scan the QR code or visit

www.themindshifteffect.com

References

Abramson, Ashley. "Cultivating Empathy." *American Psychological Association*, November 1, 2021, https://www.apa.org/monitor/ 2021/11 /feature-cultivating-empathy.

Ahmadi (Soroush), Hadi. "Facilitating Change Management with Kotter's 8-step Model." *ITSM Tools*, 20 July 2023, https://itsm.tools/kotter-change-management/.

Bosworth, Pat. "The Power of Good Communication in the Workplace." *Leadership Choice*, 2016. https://leadership choice.com/power-good-communication-workplace/.

Bryan, Lowell. "Enduring Ideas: The 7-S Framework." *McKinsey Quarterly,* 1 Mar. 2008, www.mckinsey.com/capabilities/strategy-and-corporate-finance/our-insights/enduring-ideas-the-7-s-framework.

Clayton, Sarah Jensen. "An Agile Approach to Change Management." *Harvard Business Review*, 11 Jan. 2021, hbr.org/2021/01/an-agile-approach-to-change-management.

Creasey, Tim. "Primary Sponsor's Role and Importance." *Prosci*, updated 14 March 2024, www.prosci.com/blog/primary-sponsors-role-and-importance#:~:text= Senior%20leaders%20are%20the%20preferred,direct%20engagement%20with%20impacted%20employees.

"DMAIC: Approach to Continuous Improvement 2024." *Six Sigma*, 2024, www.6sigma.us/dmaic-process/.

Duhigg, Charles. "What Google Learned From Its Quest to Build the Perfect Team." The New York Times Magazine, 25 Feb. 2016, www.nytimes.com/2016/02/28/magazine/what-google-learned-from-its-quest-to-build-the-perfect-team.html.

Dweck, Carol S. Mindset: The New Psychology of Success. Random House, 2007.

Gallo, Amy. "What Is Psychological Safety?" *Harvard Business Review*, 15 Feb. 2023, https://hbr.org/2023/02/what-is-psychological-safety.

Gu, Zhenjing, et al. "Impact of Employees' Workplace Environment on Employees' Performance: A Multi-Mediation Model." *National Library of Medicine*, 13 May 2022.

Hunt, Dame Vivian, et al. "Diversity Matters Even More: The Case for Holistic Impact." *McKinsey & Company*, 5 Dec. 2023, www.mckinsey.com/featured-insights/diversity-and-inclusion/diversity-matters-even-more-the-case-for-holistic-impact.

Hussain, Syed Talib et al. "Kurt Lewin's change model: A critical review of the role of leadership and employee involvement in organizational change." *Science Direct: Journal of Innovation & Knowledge*, vol. 3, no. 3, 2018, www.sciencedirect.com/ science/article /pii/S2444569X1630 0087.

Keller, Scott. "High-Performing Teams: A Timeless Leadership Topic." *McKinsey Quarterly*, 28 June 2017, https://www.mckinsey.com/capabilities/people-and-organizational-performance/our-insights/high-performing-teams-a-timeless-leadership-topic.

Laranjo, L. "Social Media and Health Behavior Change. Participatory Health Through Social Media", 2016. *ScienceDirect*, https://www.sciencedirect.com/topics/ social-sciences/goal-setting-theory.

Lencioni, Patrick M. The Ideal Team Player: How to Recognize and Cultivate the Three Essential Virtues. 2016.

Loc, Daniel. "30+ Change Management Statistics in 2024: A Glimpse into the Landscape of Change." Daniel Lock Consulting, 1 Mar. 2024, https://daniellock.com/change-management-statistics/#ib-toc-anchor-0.

Lonczak, Heather S., and Anna Katharina Schaffner, Ph.D. "Positive Reinforcement in the Workplace (Incl. 90+ Examples)." *Positive Psychology*, 9 Apr. 2019, positivepsychology.com/ positive-reinforcement-workplace/.

Mind Tools Content Team. "Amabile and Kramer's Progress Theory: Using Small Wins to Enhance Motivation." *Mind Tools*, www.mindtools.com/arzm8fy/amabile-and-kramers-progress-theory.

Moore, Catherine. "How to Apply Appreciative Inquiry: A Visual Guide." *PositivePsychology.com*, 21 May 2019, www.positivepsychology.com/appreciative-inquiry-visual-guide/. Scientifically reviewed by Jo Nash, Ph.D.

"New Research Shows Companies Built for the Future Are Generating Shareholder Returns Almost Three Times Greater Than Those of the S&P 1200." *BCG*, 4 Apr. 2023, www.bcg.com/press/4april2023-companies-built-for-future-shareholder-returns-three-times-greater.

O'Connor, Cliodhna. "The Brain in Society: Public Engagement with Neuroscience." *Academia*, 2013, www.academia.edu/ 7362200/The_brain_in_society_ Public_engagement_with_neuroscience.

"Prosci ADKAR Model: A powerful yet simple model for facilitating individual change." *Prosci*, www.prosci.com/methodology/adkar.

Scott, Kim. "How to Juggle Praise and Criticism and Why You Should Avoid the Feedback Sandwich." *Radical Candor*, https://www.radicalcandor.com/ blog/feedback-sandwich-praisecriticism/#:~:text=Folks%20who%20receive%20the%20feedback,the%20other%20person%20retained%20it.

Sorenson, Susan. "The Benefits of Employee Engagement." Gallup, 20 June 2013, updated 7 January 2023, www.gallup.com/workplace/236927/employee-engagement-drives-growth.aspx.

Soyer, Emre, and Robin M. Hogarth. "Don't Learn the Wrong Lessons from Failure." *Harvard Business Review*, 29 Mar. 2023, hbr.org/2023/03/dont-learn-the-wrong-lessons-from-failure.

Taylor, Dylan. "Council Post: Active Listening and Empathy for Better Working Relationships." *Forbes*, Forbes Magazine, 31 July 2023, www.forbes.com/sites/forbesbusinesscouncil/2023/07/28/active-listening-and-empathy-for-better-working-relationships/?sh=15a532cc15f6. Accessed 21 Apr. 2024.

"The Transparency Paradox: Could Less Be More When It Comes to Trust?" *Deloitte Insights*, Deloitte, 5 Feb. 2024, www2.deloitte.com/us/en/insights/ focus/human-capital-trends/2024/transparency-in-the-workplace.html. Accessed 21 Apr. 2024.

"Team Stage, Project Management Statistics: Trends and Common Mistakes in 2024." *Team Stage*, 2024, teamstage.io/project-management-statistics/.

Wu, Andy, et al. "4 Types of Innovators Every Organization Needs." *Harvard Business Review,* 27 Oct. 2022, hbr.org/2022/10/4-types-of-innovators-every-organization-needs.

www.ingramcontent.com/pod-product-compliance
Lightning Source LLC
Chambersburg PA
CBHW052148220526
45471CB00004B/1579